HEAR OUR PRAYERS AND HYMNS,

O LORD, WE PRAY

OCCASIONAL PRAYERS INVOCATIONS
PASTORAL PRAYERS DEDICATIONS
OF OFFERINGS
BENEDICTIONS

AND

LYRICS

BY

DANIEL J. THERON
M.A., B.D.Th./Ph.D.

1stBooks – rev. 6/12/01

Sitting: E.P. Groenewald, M.A., Th.D. (Amsterdam),
G.M. Pellissier, B.A., B.D. (London) - Dean.
Standing: J.H. Kritzinger, M.A., Th.D (Amsterdam),
D.J. Keet, B.A. (Oxford), Th.D. (Amsterdam)

DEDICATED TO THE
MEMORY OF

G. M. PELLISSIER

D. J. KEET

AND J. H. KRITZINGER

AND TO

E. P. GROENEWALD

FIRST PROFESSORS OF THE THEOLOGICAL FACULTY,
SECTION B,
UNIVERSITY OF PRETORIA,
REPUBLIC OF SOUTH AFRICA

TABLE OF CONTENTS

LYRICS

TO THE READERS

Prayer, one might say, is the fourth dimension of human existence, a dimension of mystery-a spiritual dimension, for God is Spirit, and God dwells in us as Spirit. This dimension becomes especially manifest in silent prayer, whether it is done privately or corporately. It is noteworthy that we do not lip our words when engaged in silent prayer. Instead, we pray in unexpressed thought. Yet, we believe that we make contact with the Almighty. In vocal prayers, on the other hand, because we are human, rightly, or in error, the truth of God being Spirit drops into the background, and we resort to anthropomorphic terms. As humans we have no choice, and there is nothing wrong with it. It is the way we have been created.

Prayer, to begin with and to end with, is essentially a very private matter. It is a communication between an individual and God, the Almighty. Even pastoral prayers are prayers of the clergy on behalf of themselves and on behalf of those whom they lead in worship and prayer.

When we think of God as Spirit, we begin to realize how inscrutable, how ineffable God truly is, how wholly other than human beings. Attributes we assign to him are merely anthropomorphic terms needed to have some understanding of the great mystery of the Almighty.

Therefore, in prayer, we as humans assume access to God in a spiritual relationship; that God as Spirit is near us, even in us; that God hears us and listens to our prayers, whether the prayer is adoration, confession, or supplication; that God will answer, not always in our time and on our terms; that those who pray, do their own part; that prayer is a means of comfort, and ease; that prayer is a means of inspiration.

Inspiration of prayer rests on the awesome assumption that God as Spirit dwells in us. So, in a sense hard for us fully to fathom and to understand, prayer is also directed to the suppliant, to the one who prays, for we are coworkers of God in our own lives and in this world.

There is great danger that prayers become stereotyped and meaningless routines, as unfortunately is often the case with grace at meals that are often rambled off in a hurry. How many times has a father said: "Let us pray," and a child would pipe up, "But

Dad, we already did." Dad might even shake the family up by paying attention to his prayer, and once in a while using an entirely different grace.

Even in pastoral prayers, repetition of the same thoughts, and particularly of the same wording, can lull both pastor and worshiper to slumbers, and complacency, no matter how beautiful the prayers may be. This is especially the case when a prayer is given, so to speak, "from the heart." Prayers that become stereotyped usually have lost their originally intended inspiration, feeling, and even sincerity in their presentation.

The purpose of this book of prayers is by no means to provide a substitute for individual, or group, or pastoral prayers. A prayer can be inspirational and thought provoking. Or a prayer could provide ideas for prayers to those who hear or read it. It is hoped that these prayers will be used to these ends and more as well.

However, there are people who at times are called upon, or who may desire to lead in prayer. But they are handicapped for whatever reason and find it difficult to do so extemporaneously. It often ends up in embarrassment for all. For them, by all means, use a written prayer.

Some of the prayers are of necessity rather long, but are put together in such a way that individual paragraphs can be lifted from them and used as shorter prayers, appropriate to various occasions.

Many of the shorter prayers in this collection had their origins in prayers to open meetings of the Simsbury and Hartford Civitan Clubs in Connecticut, and of the New England Civitan International District meetings over many years while serving as Chaplain. Civitan is a non-sectarian, international organization with a lofty creed. Consequently, many prayers reflect its inter-religious outreach, and also reflect the wideness of God's mercy to mankind. They were prepared purposely to avoid the dulling effect of stereotyped graces and opening prayers. It was always felt that opening prayers at meetings, like invocations at worship services, are most important for stimulation, inspiration, and tone setting for meetings that follow.

Many of these prayers, or paragraphs from them, can be used as preliminaries to a few short, appropriate sentences added at the end either for grace at a meal, or to include the purposes of a meeting and to give thanks for food and fellowship.

*   *   *   *   *

Our world has shrunk in recent times due to the amazing advancements in communication and travel. Thus one finds that often non-sectarian prayers are called for when people of different religious persuasions belong to and meet in the same organization. This in a minor way brings to mind the united and heroic sacrifice made by the four unforgettable chaplains of different religious orientations who gave their life jackets to servicemen who had left their own below deck. Joined together in prayer they went to their graves in the cold Atlantic Ocean when the Dorchester was sunk during World War II.

With this smaller world, shrunken as it is today, and becoming more and more a confusion and cacophony of so many religious voices, as has been the case in the time when Christianity came to the rescue, one has often wondered whether we have perhaps already reached, or at least are standing at the doorstep of what the Apostle Paul in his time so aptly called "the fullness of time."

For centuries sages of different religious communions have been trying to scale a spiritual mountain, so much higher and so much more formidable than Mount Everest, in search of the Almighty and revelation, and have lived fruitfully by the light granted them in this endless and lofty search. If indeed we are once again living in a "fullness of time" in the history of humanity and religion, especially the Christian religion, it is sincerely prayed that the lead will come out of the treasures of Christianity, unless-dread the thought-we would be found wanting and unworthy in the judgment of the Almighty.

Prayer is universal, as the Civitan Creed states, and as its members repeat in unison: "My mouth . . . speaks prayers in every tongue." It is therefore hoped that people of different religious communions would feel comfortable with most of these prayers and adapt them to their own needs. Prayer is never perfect or complete as signified in many prayers that end with a hiatus of four periods ...., preceding the Amen. A user can add here whatever is deemed appropriate.

*   *   *   *   *

The shorter prayers were originally, seldom read, although a prayer can be read with great effect, if

xii

need be. In most cases they were committed to writing and simply used as a memory reference. In some instances prayers were written down after they had been given, but there was always preparation beforehand, which is so essential.

Prayers can come to people at odd times. Some of these prayers were first written out while commuting by bus, some in quiet meditation waiting for a church service to start, and some even when sitting down as a business man at my office desk before a busy day would start; sometimes on odd pieces of paper that happened to be at hand-the back of an envelope, a piece of promotional material, or even on a copy of a to be discarded order ticket-anything that had space on it to write on; sometimes even in the middle of the night. Discipline is needed to write thoughts down when they come to us, or they can be lost in the rush of life.

Pastoral prayers have a prominent place in the worship service next to Scripture reading and the sermon. Clergy spend days preparing sermons, delivered to people. They are often gifted with words and phrases, and consequently subject to the common temptation to go on and on with the pastoral prayer until it finally loses its intended, silent participation of the worshipers.

If one tends to yield to the temptation of stretching pastoral prayers out too long, it might be wise to write them out as part of the preparation for worship services. And once this is done, stick to the text. This will help weed out repetition of clichés Sunday after Sunday that easily become meaningless. Because of its brevity the pastoral prayer warrants a great deal of preparation.

Some people might be appalled by the very thought of committing a prayer to writing, simply because in their traditions it has never been done, and inspiration on the spot by the Spirit is always claimed, we hope. Just a brief reminder: The prayer, probably used most of all prayers, is a written prayer. Of course, I mean The Lord's Prayer.

Unfortunately, God does not reward laziness, neither in sermons, nor in prayers. Once a bold pastor, quoting Scripture, announced that henceforth he would no longer prepare his sermons beforehand, but would rely solely on the Holy Spirit in the pulpit. When asked a few weeks later about his recent preaching success, he said, "Yes, but it was a brief sermon." Pressed for the content, he finally confessed: "The Holy Spirit said: 'Hans, you are lazy.'"

Spur-of-the-moment prayers are at times surprisingly inspiring, most likely because such are rooted in a life of prayer and adequate preparation of prayers when needed at other times to build up a reservoir from which to draw. But often, spur-of-the-moment prayers are fleeting and just as non-lasting as the moment in which they are given.

Days are spent preparing sermons delivered to people. Why not spend time preparing prayers for talking to God on behalf of his people?

There is the danger that the worship service through the centuries has become stale and dry with the same invocation and the same benediction, worship service after worship service. It is like a well known sentence between quotation marks. The important element of wide awake anticipation is missing.

Benedictions can be subject to the same pitfalls as prayers. We have become so accustomed to our traditional benedictions that they easily end up stereotyped, and lose a great deal of their intended significance at the end of the worship service, as if just a customary habit of bringing it to a close, almost as if just saying: "Go home now and have lunch." In reality the service should work up to a high point in the pronouncement of the benediction. Variety can be most valuable here.

A benediction is not a prayer. However, unordained persons should use a benediction as a prayer: "May the Lord bless you ...." But for ordained clergy a benediction is an authoritative pronouncement. They are empowered with this authority by virtue of their ordination to speak for God to his people. Not a wimpy little prayer, but a powerful crescendo, ending the service to comfort, stimulate, and inspire the congregation about to pour out and do God's work in the world: "The Lord bless you and keep you ....AMEN!!" [IT IS SO!!]

It is with trepidation that the author enters the hallowed sanctuary of traditional benedictions, revered through the centuries. And this was not done lightly, nor on the spur of the moment-and never should be-but with deep reverence, as well as with thought and meditation beforehand. It is with such an attitude that the author even dares to suggest a few benedictions that he believes could enhance the conclusion of a worship service and help lift worship services out of a rut that often contributes to dullness and unfruitfulness.

The grouping of prayers by months should be taken quite loosely. The Table of Contents should be helpful to locate topics.

Music expresses many moods in our lives and in a worship service. It was not until recent years that the author attempted to put some thoughts in verse form and adapted them to fit existing music, for singing together is an uplifting and inspiring form of worship. It is a dimension of fellowship that far exceeds reading in unison, or anything else that a congregation or group of people can engage in together.

The author would be remiss in not expressing his gratitude to artists, C. A. De Morest, the late Theodore H. Robinson, and William L. Wheeler, all of Hendersonville, NC for the sketches that they made to add interest to various prayers, as well as to Beverly A. Ward, Ralph Morris, and Doedy Polk, all of Hendersonville, NC whose advice was invaluable in helping to suit lyrics to melodies and also preparing the music texts. A special word of thanks to Linda Harney, Hendersonville, NC for proofreading. However, the author wishes to state that none of those who contributed their expertise should in any way be held responsible for any shortcomings of the book.

Prayers belong to all of us. Therefore, if a person, lay or clergy, should feel led to use any of the prayers, invocations, pastoral prayers, offering prayers, and benedictions in this collection for public use in worship, or other occasions, he or she is free to do so. Of course, copyright rules would prevail for reproduction of all or part of this book.

It is sincerely hoped that it would be an inspiration to the reader.

The Author
Hendersonville, NC
December 14, 2000

JANUARY

A Pilgrim's Prayers

1

Lord, our God, when the mountains and hills before us are steep and not made low, let your presence be our staff and strength to surmount and to conquer.

When disappointments obstruct our ways, empower us with courage and insight to turn them into stepping stones leading to unknown opportunities.

When the impossible confronts us, grant us visions and dreams of hope to renew our inspiration.

When the crooked on our journey is not made straight, be our compass lest we lose our way.

When rough places are not made plain, provide us with shoes to continue our pilgrimage without pain or fear.

When the valleys of life are deep and not made level, and all seems to fail, grant us wings to mount up like eagles, we pray....Amen.

2

O Lord, during our sojourn on earth, let despondence never be our master, for you are always near. Merciful Lord, as life is sometimes mingled with tears of sorrow, mourning, and struggle, but often also brightened by smiles of accomplishment, satisfaction, and contentment, grant us a victorious conclusion to our pilgrimage. Transform all of our experiences on earth into one melody of happiness and laughter that in the end there may break upon our spirits that distant, long awaited, triumph song of eternity, a new commencement of joy and service forever, we pray....Amen.

The Open Door of a New Beginning

Almighty God, our Father, as we begin a new year, we thank you that you have so fashioned creation and our own lives as to always confront us with the challenge of new and unknown frontiers.

We thank you for the new frontiers of our time: the electronic age, the nuclear age, the space age, the age of wonder drugs, and the age of genetic engineering. We stand as insignificant, little people before the irresistible beckoning of these overwhelming frontiers of our lives. As beneficiaries of these marvelous discoveries of your handiwork, bestow upon us, the people of your creation, a double portion of the sense of our own responsibility, lasting values of integrity, humility, love, and moral stamina, lest we become arrogant, and destroy ourselves with the gifts of vast knowledge that you have intended to be of endless benefit to us.

As you guide us into the new year and as we cross the threshold of the unknown, the unexplored, and the unexpected, may your light always be a lamp unto our feet, lest we stumble and fall.

By your light that illumined the world through the wise and dedicated of the past transform us into the light of the world ourselves, set on a hill, that can not be hid, that peace and goodwill may reign on the earth, we pray....Amen.

Excelsior!

Grant us, O Lord, the wisdom and confidence to know
That the shadows in life here below
Are only your Kingdom's flag up higher,
Waving with the clarion: Excelsior, Excelsior!
....Amen.

Ora et Labora

Grant, O Lord, that we shall not only make our desires known to you in our prayers, but that we shall also discipline ourselves and work unceasingly and diligently so that our labors will become part of the answers to our prayers, for you have summoned us in this life, not only to be your servants, but also to be your colaborers....Amen.

3

Spiritual Growth

Dear Lord, implant and nourish within us the high resolve and ability to grow and to become mature and strong. Liberate us from the fear or unwillingness of climbing out of the cradle. Liberate us from the immaturity that refuses to grow beyond being fed with milk, lest we languish, remain soft, and live as children when we should mature to full manhood and womanhood in our relationship with you and with our fellow human beings.

Hear Our Prayers And Hymns, O Lord, We Pray

And once out of the nursery, Dear Lord, enable us to continue to grow lest we languish in staleness; enable us to continue to grow lest we degenerate and decay; enable us to grow lest we become spiritually old.

Open the depth of your mysteries that our hearts and our roots may tap into the springs of living water that are continually refreshed by your presence.

So enable us to mature like giants in the forest season after season renewing our hearts and our minds, that we may flourish from strength to strength, even into eternity....Amen.

The Comfort of God's Presence

Almighty God, our Father, in our universe and on the earth in which we live, you have made us part of time and of eternity. As in your mercy we find ourselves once again at the portals of a new year, we thank you, despite the vastness of your creation, that we are never alone; that you are as close to us as the touch of our hands, as the sight of our eyes, as the sound in our ears, as fragrance and taste in our senses, and above all, that you are not only close to us, but within us, even as you created us and continue to dwell in us and to speak to us.

As we venture into a new year, remove from our hearts and our minds, we pray, the mist and the tumult of daily living that may obscure from us the comfort of your nearness and indwelling in us. And so grant us the sure confidence that we shall never fear the unknown, even if it should hold pain, disappointment, and sorrow. Strengthen us with the conviction that you have prepared a solace for us and a solution for every untoward condition of life.

As we walk into the new year, inspire us always to anticipate the rainbow, not only after, but even while thunder is raging; to hope for light even before the dawn breaks; not only to look for, but even to search for the good around us, and especially in others.

Make us eager, we pray, to remember the times of joy in our own lives, to appropriate for ourselves the happiness and cheer around us, and above all to spread it like fragrance of flowers along life's way for others to enjoy.

"Guide us, O thou Great Jehovah, pilgrims through this barren land," we pray....Amen.

The Challenge of the Future

Almighty God, we thank you that there is so much in the history of mankind of which we can truly be proud. But we confess that there is also so much of which we should be ashamed. As we face the unknown future, make us more aware that the world and the universe belong to you, that you are always near, and that your will must be done. Enable us to learn from the challenges of the past, in which we have failed, to take up the challenges of the present with undaunted courage. So inspire us, we pray, to shape the destinies of mankind and of the world in accordance with the dictates of your Kingdom....Amen.

Hear Our Prayers And Hymns, O Lord, We Pray
Acceptable before God

O God, whose holiness is beyond our comprehension, so cleanse our desires and so direct our motives that we may truly become acceptable in your sight-a holy priesthood to you. We would bow before your requirements and your admonitions. Despite our many deficiencies and shortcomings, bring our small abilities to fruition and to a glorious issue. To that end, Lord, enable us to love others even as you love all your children; make us compassionate even as you are compassionate; teach us to understand rather than to condemn; grant us a spirit of forgiveness, even as you are willing to forgive the contrite heart. So equip us, we pray, that in love, in word, and in deed, we may be worthy to be your ambassadors in the world. ....Amen.

Confession in Time of War
(Iraqi War, January, 1991)

Almighty God, whose will is peace and brotherhood among your children, we confess our human frailty and shortcomings that mislead us to struggle through valleys of pain and suffering, and even wars, rather than to scale together the peaks of tranquility, brotherhood, and peace.

We confess the evil of war, whether we can justify it or not; the expenditure of vast amounts of our substance to attack enemies of flesh and blood, those who should be our brethren; exposing your children and nations to the ravages of war and ourselves and coming

7

generations to moral decadence that armed conflict generates in our midst.

We confess ignoring that the strife of your Kingdom is not against flesh and blood, but against the evil desires of darkness that lurk in the human heart.

We confess not girding ourselves with the armor of righteousness against greed and want that make for jealousy and enmity, which in turn cause nation to rise up against nation.

We confess how little we tax ourselves for the cause of your Kingdom; not encouraging our sons and daughters to labor in the fields of your Kingdom as lay people, or as ministers and missionaries of your good tidings to change the hearts of people that peace may reign among nations. Instead we have often sacrificed them as cannon and missile fodder on the battle fields of the world.

For these shortcomings forgive us, O Lord, we pray. As you pardon us in your endless mercy, grant that all people shall grow in your grace and respond with grateful hearts, and above all, hearts, willing to be changed....Amen.

Inner Peace

Almighty God, we thank you that in spite of arms races, in spite of wars, terrorism, bloodshed, and tears there is a peace that surpasses all understanding-your peace.

Bestow upon us that peace, we pray, in the knowledge that you are not only the father of us all, regardless of race, color, or creed, but also Lord over us all, Lord of history and Lord of human destiny.

Whatever our lot may be, we rejoice in the secure refuge of your providence. For your fatherly care that hovers over us and over all of your creation, we give thanks....Amen.

Leaders of the World

Almighty God, our Father, your dominion is over all the earth and over all its people, and only at your bidding are there rulers, kings, queens, presidents, prime ministers, others chosen as representatives, and even self-appointed dictators, to hold dominion over the nations and peoples of the world.

We thank you for the ability and the urge of many who aspire to the high office of leadership; for their willingness to sacrifice lives of privacy and ease, and to be subjected to scrutiny, criticism, and even ridicule in the exercise of their duties; for their commitment to make the momentous decisions for their own, and also for other nations.

In quiet moments with themselves and under the searchlight of conscience, grant them to know that their elevation to high office is but a summons and a trust from the highest authority to humility of service, service not only to those whom you have placed under their rule, but above all to you. Safeguard them from the desire to dominate, from the folly of the lust for ever greater and greater power. Protect them from corruption that the power of high office and the temptation and influence of money stir in all of us. So may they be benign and just rulers of all, be they rich or poor, privileged or disadvantaged that tranquility of contentment may be the source of happiness, we pray....Amen.

2

Lord of all and over all, grant the rulers of the world an awareness of the heavy burdens resting upon their shoulders-armaments of mass destruction which may visit, war, death, bloodshed, and tears upon mankind. And with this awesome awareness grant them also the ability, we pray, to use the unusual power entrusted to them with moderation, mercy, and justice. In their dealing with nations plagued by greed, or burdened by the suffering and discontent of want that cause nation to rise up and rage against nation, grant them firmness, and high resolve of wisdom that only you can impart to establish what is right and equitable.

Let the beauty of the earth and all the fullness thereof inspire them to know that it belongs to you, that the whole world is in your hand, and that they are but servants to use it wisely and to preserve its splendor.

Grant vision, we pray, to those who rule the world, lest their people perish. So possess them that the laws by which they govern shall be exceeded only by their examples of noble and strong character, examples of integrity, and by conduct acceptable to you. Grant especially, we ask, that they shall be instruments of the supreme law of your Kingdom, the law of love. So may peace, liberty, justice, and tranquility be the comfort for all your people who dwell on the face of the earth.

Hear Our Prayers And Hymns, O Lord, We Pray

Bless, inspire, guide, and direct the leaders of our nation and our world, we beseech you, O Lord. Grant that through them, even if only in some small way, your Kingdom may come, and that above all, to your peerless name, Great Ruler of all, there shall be all honor, and praise, and glory in this world. ....Amen.

God in History

O God, the fool may say in his heart that there is no God. But we thank you that the revelation of your glory in the world is unmistakable and that it did not come to an end with holy writ, but that you are still speaking to us even more forcefully today, if we would but observe and listen: in the whisper of electricity, in the marvels of space, in the thunder of nuclear power, in wonder drugs, in genetic engineering, in the increasing knowledge of your creation so wondrously fashioned, and in the writings, words, and works of wise men and women through the circling years.

We stand in awe at your great majesty, ceaselessly made known to us in the history of the past, in the works of your hands surrounding us, and above all, by your presence in us. We can not but come to you with gratitude and thanksgiving for the beauty of this planet which you have created as our home, but also for so much that makes life enjoyable....Amen.

FEBRUARY

The Loss of a Child or Loved One

Father of us all, you create our children. With joy we receive them, nourish and cherish them as our own, a divine, sacred trust from you. But death may cruelly and unexpectedly take one away, as it often takes other loved ones also. In our pain of grief and in our tears of sorrow, enlighten us to understand, and undergird us to be comforted in the assurance that what you have created remains forever and truly never dies. For even out of the ashes of a lowly plant, consumed by fire, there can rise a mighty tree; how much more out of the death of a loved one.

Hard, incomprehensible, and sorrowful as it may be, speak to us clearly as only a loving father can that we may accept that you have lent us, if only for a short time, a precious one to safe keep for you until at your own bidding the moment had arrived to commence a homeward journey.

Even though too brief for our commitment of love, comfort us that we have had the joy and privilege of safekeeping your child in this world for you. Comfort us further, we pray, in the assurance that death is not a devastation and not the end of great expectations, dreams, and ideals that we have conceived and cherished to accomplish for the one that we have now lost, but that our fondest dreams and expectations are ever in your hands, hands so much stronger than ours could ever have been.

Thank you for the comfort of imagination that we may enjoy the pleasures of tender memories that will ever remain with us, for the treasure of love never dies.

We would rely on your everlasting and sustaining arms, always under and around us all, whether we live, or whether we die, arms so much more loving and providing than we could ever have hoped to supply ourselves.

And now, O Lord, as we seek your comfort turn tears, sorrow, and mourning into a blessing. Transform our hope into assurance of a song triumphant at the end of life's distant rainbow, we pray....Amen.

Creators in our Own Lives

Almighty God, our Father, we thank you that out of chaos and many contrasts you have created a universe of grandeur, and fashioned our planet in harmony and in unspeakable beauty and splendor.

We thank you that your indwelling in us connects us with the unfathomable source of creativity to become creators in our own lives.

Enable us, we pray, creators of our own little worlds, in the midst of the chaos of our day, and in the midst of the contrasts of pain and delight, of tears and of laughter, in and around us, to fashion a haven of contentment, of trust, of harmony, and of beauty.

May your presence so well up in us, we pray, that we may strive to be master creators ourselves. Bountifully bestow upon us a full measure of wisdom and your divine guidance every day that the imaginations of our minds, the inspiration and love of our hearts, and the work of our minds may build a haven of peace and tranquility around us wherever we may find ourselves for honor and praise to you, the great master creator of all....Amen.

Confidence

1

Almighty God, grant us the confidence that comes from knowing that you are our Father. Renew in us the faith of your unfailing providence.

Even as you have supplied abundantly in all our needs of yesterday and of this day, so vouchsafe to us the assurance that you will also supply in our wants of tomorrow, the day after, and forever, even into eternity....Amen.

2

Almighty God, our Father, as each day is but a small threshold of the great unknown and sometimes of a threatening and uncertain future, grant that we shall not fear darkness, or tempest, or lightning, or thunder that may beset our lives, because your presence is a lamp unto our feet, and a shelter when we are beset by a storm in life....Amen.

Daniel J. Theron

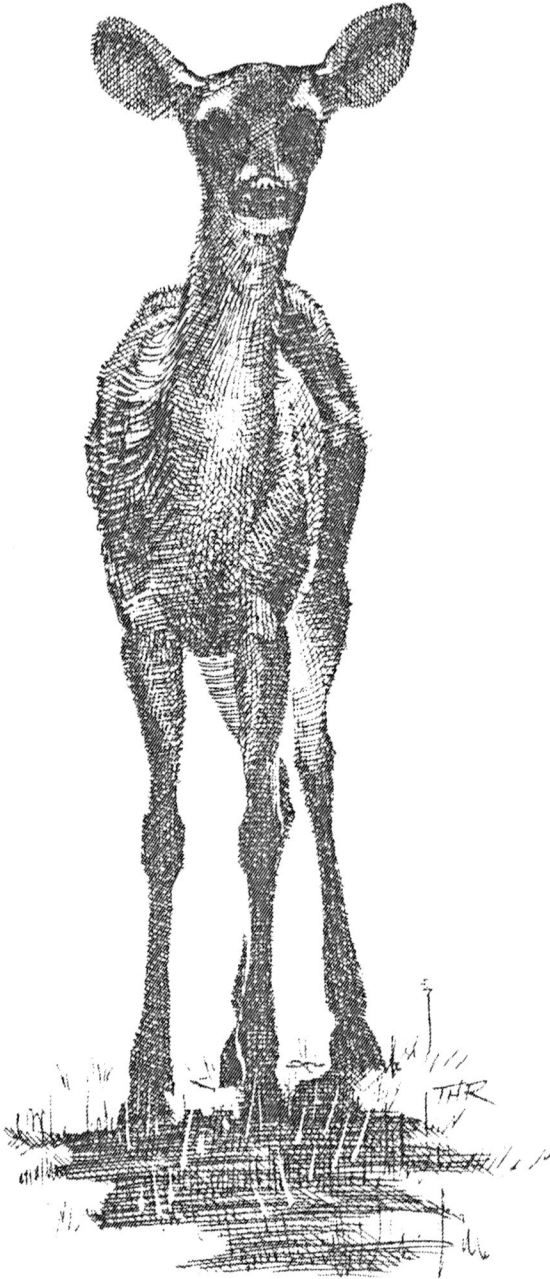

Divine Providence

Almighty God, Father of all, you are indeed the giver of every good and perfect gift. Your providence is manifest in all things around us. The swallow finds a place to build a nest for its young and the lowly sparrow satisfies itself even when there seems to be nothing. The gentle fawn survives the harshness of winter. At your appointed time, new life springs from what had seemed to have perished, the earth is refreshed and brings forth the tender blade, the plant, and the harvest.

We thank you for confidence that, even as you provide in the needs of nature, so will you also supply in our own needs, not only of material things, but above all of things unseen, spiritual, and eternal ....Amen.

Security

Lord, our God, protect us, we pray, from the arrow the flies by night and from the pestilence that walks in darkness, for these we can not see, and against these we can not safeguard ourselves, be it physical harm, or disease that may threaten our bodies.

As we rely on you for our physical safety, point us to a security that is far more important, a security that is not tied to material things, but to the unseen. Protect us from the arrow and the pestilence that are aimed at what is eternal, and seek to destroy faith, love, and hope, that these may remain and be strengthened as our shield and protection in all conditions of life, even in facing the mysteries beyond....Amen.

When the Shadows of Life are Lengthening

Almighty God, our Father, we thank you for the most precious gift that you have graciously bestowed upon us-the gift of life;

For the tenaciousness implanted in our bodies and in our minds to cling to that life and to survive even devastating trauma and illness;

For interests, faith, hope, and vision that sustain life;

For genes that enable many of us to live far beyond three score years and ten;

For the marvels of the age of wonder drugs and surgery that enable us to lengthen and to enjoy life;

For the many years of happiness and good health that countless numbers of us can enjoy in spite of advanced age.

But when the gift of genes, the marvels of medicine, and the skills of surgery begin to fail, and life of advanced age becomes a burden and a cross-sometimes with pain and suffering-grant us the faith, the willingness, the skills, the grace, and the strength to bear that cross cheerfully, and boldly, and even to support others who may have to bear crosses of their own. Grant us human companionship to help bear whatever burdens may come our way. Above all, make us aware that you are our constant companion, all the time.

Daniel J. Theron

We thank you for happy memories and humor of days gone by that brighten our lives over and over again, even when we are alone;

For the comforting and lasting satisfaction of our accomplishments in life;

For the company of loved ones and friends that sustain us;

For the joy of seeing the future in new generations, following in our footsteps.

And as the shadows of life are lengthening, and as our path on earth gets steeper every day, be our rod and our staff; and in the end, O Lord, be our eternal home, we pray....Amen.

Evening

1

Almighty God, our Father, as the clamor and the noise of this day are silenced in the hush of eventide, make us aware of things eternal that transcend our daily cares. As the purple of the mountains and hills deepens into darkness under the glory of the firmament, and as the lights of the heavenly host are illumined far, far beyond, grant us comfort in your infinite majesty and power surrounding us and providing in our daily wants. We are thankful for the abundance of your providence, sufficient for all our needs, not only of the day now at rest, but also of the night to come, and forever....Amen.

Almighty God, our Father,

For the task of life entrusted to us;

For inspiration to meet its challenge each day;

For the call and strength to fulfill our daily duty;

But also for the call now to pause in the

Peace and quiet of eventide that we may be renewed;

For rest in satisfaction of our day's task done well,

We close this day-whatever it brought to us-with

Thanksgiving and gratitude to you....Amen.

Service

Almighty God, you have set a purpose before each of us, as we set out and as we continue our pilrimage of life. We thank you that we can be your coworkers in the world.

Grant that our eyes will be your eyes to see the wrongs in the world around us; that our ears will be your ears to hear the cries for help; that our hands will be your hands to do your work while it is day; that our feet will be your feet along the dusty roads and highways, swift and hastening even upon the mountains to bring tidings of joy and happiness.
....Amen.

The Call to Special Duty

Almighty God, our Father, we thank you that through the ages you have called men and women to higher duties among their fellow human beings; that you have spoken to the lad Samuel in the quiet of night and made him your spokesman among his people; that you have called the Apostle Paul in a dazzling light and violent fall from his steed to become the most important religious missionary and theologian of the Christian Church; that you have called Thomas Aquinas to be a guide to his Church; that you have called Martin Luther in the thunder of lightning to devote his life to higher service; that you have called Mother Theresa and a host of others throughout history to be your hands among suffering people.

We thank you for millions from many faiths of the world, whom you have called through the ages and who have heeded your voice, who have surrendered all, but to follow the dictates of your call, bringing your word to your people, touching and transforming their hearts and lives to be in tune with your will and love for your children.

We thank you that higher duty is not necessarily going through years of theological training and standing in a pulpit, or at a lectern, but comes to all of us in our ordinary, daily walks of life: to be good people, equipped with wisdom and great hearts, to give a cup of cold water, to speak a kind and comforting word, to have a sense of humor, to be your representatives, your eyes, your ears, your hands, your feet, your voice on the highways, in the alleys, and on the dusty footpaths of this world; wherever we are, in our own imperfect way, to be God to people.

That your purposes may be fulfilled on earth renew in all of us the spirit of your call to the duty of service, we pray....Amen.

Hear Our Prayers And Hymns, O Lord, We Pray

*The Four Chaplains**

---

*The SS *Dorchester* was on its way in a convoy from
Newfoundland to Greenland. On the fateful, early morning of
February 3, 1942 it was torpedoed by a German U-boat,
striking it near the engine room on the starboard side. The
time was 0355 GCT. The engines were destroyed and the ship
immediately began to take on tons of water. So severely was
it damaged that it could not even inform the rest of the
convoy of the disaster that had struck it. The other ships
sailed on unaware of the tragedy in the making. Three
minutes later, at 0358 GCT, abandon ship was ordered. Many
of the men came on deck without their life jackets.

Soon there appeared on the rapidly listing deck of the
doomed ship its four chaplains: George Lansing Fox, a
Methodist, Clark Vandersall Poling, [Dutch] Reformed,
Alexander David Goode, a Jewish Rabbi, and John Patrick
Washington, a Catholic Priest. They tried to bring some
order in the confusion of that dark and bitter cold night,
handing out life jackets from a storage locker until the
supply was exhausted, and then gave away their own to the
young soldiers who had none. When the ship quickly sank at
about 0420 GCT the four chaplains stood arm in arm. As
confirmed by one who swam away just in time, they were
praying, and so perished in the frigid and wind-swept North
Atlantic waters about 150 miles west of Cape Farewell,
Greenland. 605 out of 904 aboard were lost!

These chaplains will always be near to the hearts of
their countrymen as exceptional heroes of World War II. This
sentiment is amply demonstrated in various ways: The Chapel
of the Four Chaplains, in Philadelphia (1951), a place for
interfaith worship, and The Four Chaplains Memorial
Fountain, Falls Church, Virginia (1955). In addition
Congress in 1961 voted to bestow upon each of them
posthumously a Special Medal of Heroism, the only ones ever.
The U. S. Postal Service issued a stamp in their honor.
February 3 became the Four Chaplains Observance Day. Since
1960 Civitan International, at its club meetings, has
observed Clergy Week annually in honor of these four heroes
of great faith that enabled them to make the supreme
sacrifice.

(The author is indebted to the United States Navy for
much of the information about the *Dorchester* and its demise,
chronicled above.)

Hear Our Prayers And Hymns, O Lord, We Pray

1

And on this day, especially, we give thanks to you, Almighty God, for your call to higher duty that came clearly in the lives of the four chaplains who served on the Dorchester during World War II. We would honor them as brave heroes of their faith as they stood together, united and undaunted, on the listing deck of the sinking ship that fateful, early morning hour of February 3, 1942, when it was torpedoed and sank in the cold Atlantic waters. Grant, we pray, that their examples of devotion to the duties of a higher call may be a lasting inspiration to all of us in whatever duties, sometimes even small, you assign to us to perform in life....Amen.

2

We thank you for the dedication and faithfulness of the four chaplains to the high calling which you had extended to them, for their unconditional commitment to their duty; for their undaunted determination; that for them all that counted was that greater love has no one but to lay down his life for his brother; that they could set an unforgettable, historic example of loving care, ministering to those entrusted to them by their calling; that as officers they unselfishly gave their own life jackets to young service men who were without-to whom life was still so dear, for whom the future was beckoning, even though they were willing themselves also to lay down their own lives in the call and service of their country.

For the lasting legacy of vicariously living and suffering which these chaplains have bequeathed to us we give thanks to you....Amen.

3

God, our father, we thank you that the four Chaplains, facing tempest, billows, and awaiting the throws of death, were willing, calmly and courageously, to be sacrificed on the cross of freezing ocean waves that others might be saved and live.

We thank you that, as they stood there arm in arm in prayer on the sinking Dorchester, bravely awaiting their immolation, they could demonstrate to the world that for those to whom your call of service comes irresistibly clear, there is neither Christian nor Jew, neither Protestant, nor Catholic, or any other faith, neither male nor female, but that we are all your children and your servants, united in our upward call. Therefore, for the wideness of your mercy and your love that bind us all together, we give thanks.
....Amen.

4

Almighty God, we are thankful for the honor, high esteem, and remembrance bestowed upon the four chaplains by their country and their fellow human beings in various ways.

Above all do we thank you that for them there awaited from you an honor far exceeding what mankind on earth can ever bestow-the crown of glory!
....Amen.

5

Grant, O Lord, that devastation, untimely death, suffering, bloodshed, and tears brought on by war, in such sharp contrast with the example of love, so

Hear Our Prayers And Hymns, O Lord, We Pray unselfishly given by these four chaplains, will help to hasten the day when torpedoes, and bombs, and instruments of warfare will be turned into instruments of peace to supply in the needs of your children, and that mankind will be at peace and make war no more. So may your Kingdom come....Amen.

Daniel J. Theron

MARCH

God's Inscrutable Mystery in the Universe

1

Lord, our God, we stand in awe of the beginning of this vast and unfathomable universe which you have created as you brought existence and order out of nothing and chaos. We thank you that with the marvels and beauty of your creation you surround and sustain our insignificant, little planet, earth, and even ourselves, who are but specks of dust, and but fleeting moments in the vast scheme of endless time and eternity.

We stand in awe that you are Spirit, inscrutable, inconceivable ineffable, holy and also the wholly other; that nevertheless you are willing to make yourself known to us, through your indwelling as Spirit in us that feebly, with mind and heart we can struggle in seeking you and be enriched by what you have and still are revealing to us.

We stand in awe of the mysteries, the wonders, and the deep secrets, that your power and wisdom have locked up and that have been made known to us on our small planet. We stand in awe of the wonder of the beginning of life with its tenacious continuation from generation to generation in plants, and in all that live and breathe....Amen.

God, our Father, we stand in awe of your mysterious presence so near to us, as if we can sense and touch it as our own, for from you do we come as your children. And yet, how little do we understand and truly grasp. Grant, we earnestly pray, that we shall not be smart know-it-alls.

We stand in awe of the depth of your counsel, so often so far beyond our fathoming and our understanding as we seek to lead and to order our lives from day to day.

We thank you for millions through the ages who have sought diligently in thought, meditation, and prayer to reach more fully beyond that veil of mystery that shrouds your majesty from our finite minds; for sacred Scriptures handed over to us through the ages, but still insufficient to tell us what you in reality are.

We thank you even for the primitive who, in the wideness of your mercy, have sometimes perceived openings in that veil of vast mystery of your presence around us, and who can find faith and trust, gain comfort and solace, be it even in such lowly forms of worship as might be despised by many to be ignorant and unworthy of your majesty. Nevertheless, we thank you for the little, or plenty with which, those who have heard your whispers have enriched the spiritual life of their little worlds and aided mankind to strive towards a worthy and godly conduct of their time on earth, sometimes marked by hard struggle, sometimes, by your grace, enriched with joy and laughter....Amen.

3

Lord of the progression of history, shatter for good, we pray, the know-it-all cocoons in which we can so easily and so comfortably encapsulate and ensconce ourselves to live in, cooped up for life. Liberate us like butterflies from our cocoons to soar to new heights and into an unknown experience of continuing revelation and learning, for your revelation from the other side of the veil will never be final and complete so that our finite minds and spirits can ever fully comprehend it.

Grant that the cover of mystery, surrounding us, will continue to burst open, even if only little by little in research and discovery of science, even unwittingly revealed by agnostics, or even atheists, for they too are destined to be your servants and your instruments.

As we continue to walk through the circling years along the path of life with its pitfalls, its valleys of travails and tears, or its glorious summits of high mountains with unbelievable revelation and great joy, let us never cease, we pray, to seek, to learn, and above all, to find you anew, and when we find, to hear and to listen to what you sometimes whisper, or sometimes thunder and proclaim unmistakably clear from the other side of that mysterious veil.

To you who created us, and ever urge us on and on to reach beyond and beyond until some day we shall return whence we came, and better understand, to you be all honor, and glory, and thanksgiving for ever....Amen.

Good and Evil in the World

O God, Creator of the universe and the earth, you have fashioned all in such astounding contrast of beauty, light and darkness, the colors of the rainbow, everything so masterfully woven into creation around us-too much for us to grasp. But as we marvel at your handiwork, we stand baffled by what seems to be the irreconcilable contrast of good and evil within ourselves, which we spread in the world around us.

We acknowledge and confess that the roots of evil sprout forth from within ourselves to grow into trees, fed by our misuse of gifts and desires with which you have endowed us, the gift of tenacity of life, the desires of self-preservation, gratification, and our own security. Teach us, we pray, that we can corrupt these gifts and desires to lead us into excessive coveting of material things, and to so many other attitudes that mar harmony with our fellow human beings, and above all with you. We confess that our obsession with all these things often leads to an excessive, and sometimes violent response to others, resulting in the cruelty in our midst of human being to human being, murder, the horror of infanticide, the slaughter, bloodshed, tears, and devastation of war. And as we make confession, we thank you for redemption, for cleansing, but above all that you dwell in us, calling and enabling us to join the battle against the roots of evil within ourselves and so in the world around us.

33

We thank you that the knowledge of good and evil is a mighty source of power and discipline within us to grow from strength to strength, and to overcome.

Liberate us, we pray, from imagining a super power outside of your creation and outside of ourselves that would lead us astray, and so exculpate ourselves from the wrongs that we allow to overcome us, for you are the only creator and the ultimate source of goodness, harmony, peace, and gladness.

And in the end, when our spirits return to you, grant that we shall come home as soldiers of your Kingdom, victorious over evil that has its root within ourselves; that we shall no longer see dimly in a mirror, but face to face fully learn why the contrast of good and evil was part of our lives and of our world....Amen.

Prayer for a Murderer

Almighty God, our Father, we thank you for the most precious of gifts bestowed upon mankind-the gift of life. And life being so precious, we thank you that you have set as a sentinel over us the gravity of your law, not to shed blood, not to take a life, not to kill, not to murder.

We thank you for your amazing grace extended to those who have transgressed this law and have deprived others of the splendor of life, the enjoyment thereof, and the fulfilling of their purposes for which you have created and sent them into this world. We mourn that a life taken can never be restored, that restitution can never be made. But we are thankful that only you, the giver of life, can forgive those who break your law, and take a life. Therefore, grant, we pray, that those who transgress your law not to kill will not harden their hearts, unrepentant and ignorant of the mighty power of your amazing grace.

For by your amazing grace and infinite mercy you transformed Moses, who had taken an Egyptian's life, and you made him the messenger of your law to all your people on earth, even the law, "You shall not kill."

You redeemed David, a plotter of murder, to give us the 23rd Psalm-"Tho I walk through the valley of the shadow of death, I shall fear no evil."

By your amazing grace you converted Saul, the Pharisee, who approved the stoning of Stephen, and then continued to persecute the innocent. By your amazing grace you finally made him Paul, the Apostle, to proclaim to the world that faith, hope, and love abide, but that the greatest of these is love.

Thanks be to you for your amazing grace that redeems, that makes scarlet white as snow, that saves wretches, and transforms them into mighty instruments in your hand-even saints.

"Amazing grace, how sweet the sound...." Amen.

God, our Rod and our Staff

Almighty God, Creator of all, we lift up our eyes to the hills that we have to conquer, and we too, like the Psalmist, wonder: Where is our help? When our arms grow weary and our knees falter, our vision grows dim, and our spirits despondent, enable us to say: "Our help is in the name of the Lord who made heaven and earth," for blessed is the one whose strength and

35

whose trust are in you, the source of all power and strength.

Through your power that dwells in us equip us, we pray, with such confidence and such firm resolve that will be strong enough to vanquish failure as we lean on the staff of faith for which no mountain is too steep....Amen.

Drawing Near to God

Our Father, we would look to you in prayer to acknowledge our dependence upon you and to receive from this hallowed communion with you the sustenance that we need daily to walk life's pilgrimage acceptably in your sight. Although we may regard ourselves as strong, nevertheless, we need your strength in word, thought, and deed as life goes on every day.

Whether we are favored with ease, or whether our time is consumed by our rush of life, or by our burden of toil, may we never forget to set aside time to pray, and so to renew our privileged conversation and fellowship with you that we may strengthen our constant life line with you, our unfailing source of power. To that end grant us the awareness that you, the ultimate source of strength, are always dwelling in us. So we pray....Amen.

To Be a Part of:

Lord, our God, as your presence inspires our hearts and minds, enable us truly to feel:
Part of your unfathomable creation roundabout us;
Part of the vitality throbbing and permeating the work of your hands;
Part of an unceasing quest for learning and progress;
Part of the great drama of human existence, despite all its shortcomings, its turmoil, its agony, and suffering, but also its delight, its gladness, and its joy;
Part of the healing touch extended to those in discomfort, suffering, and illness;
Part of the balm of consolation where there is sorrow;
Part of the process of reconciliation where there is animosity, enmity, or hostility;
Part of good will and making peace where there are the ravages of conflict;
Part of the helping hand where there is adversity;
Part of the great redemption that you have in store for those who come and truly seek you with all their heart;
Part of the great privilege of prayer available to those who seek your face and wait upon you;
Part of the song of rejoicing that you have in store for your children;
Part of the fulfillment of your great and glorious purposes in the world;
Co-workers with you, Creator, Sustainer, and Father of all, whose Kingdom and reign are without end!...Amen.

Daniel J. Theron

End of War

Almighty God, Ruler of all, in whose hands are the destinies of mankind, we thank you that the rising up of nation against nation has mercifully come to an end and that the thunder and violence of aircraft, missiles, and guns have echoed away into silence across now deserted battle fields.

We commend to your comfort those mourning the loss of loved ones who have perished, on whomsoever's side they might have fallen, even our enemy's side.

We pray for the maimed and mutilated, whose lives have been devastated forever. In your great goodness heal, we pray, not only the wounds in the hearts and lives of people, but also the festering wounds among factions and nations that make for hatred and unleash war.

Grant that love shall reign in the world, and bestow wisdom on all those in authority. Grant that through their deliberations and negotiations a just and lasting peace may be established, that in the end the victory shall be neither ours, nor that of the enemy, but the victory of your Kingdom in the hearts of your people.

And so, O Lord, may your Kingdom come....Amen.

Daniel J. Theron

Responsibility in the World

O Lord, as all nations are under your rule, grant that generations to come will not condemn us for too eagerly seeking and striving to be first among our peers, rather than to be part of, and one of the world.

Grant us as nations contentment with what has been allotted to us, and not to initiate aggression to have sway over others, and so to expand our own dominion, wealth, and comforts.

While we thank you for national identity, love for the flag that waves over us, pride in our own, and zeal for our country's success, enable us to respect the national pride and zeal of all other nations as well, even small, insignificant, and weak in the eyes of the world.

Where there is need, stir up, we pray, the spirit of the entrepreneur to supply in that need through exchange, commerce, and trade, lest nations resort to war and bloodshed to supply in their wants.

Grant that in the great variety of nationalities, races, religions, and creeds, we will seek and find the many common threads and ties that bind us together as your family and as part of your creation.

Grant that we shall live by the creed that you are our creator, that you dwell in each one of us, and that your love extends to all your children. Enable us to discover the common ties of love, faith, and hope for a better day that unite us all as a vast family. So enable us to inhabit our beautiful planet in peace and in a common concern one for another, and one nation for another, we pray....Amen.

APRIL

Good Friday

Our Father, we ask what is good about Good Friday?

When we were on the mountain of joy, singing and celebrating the birth of Jesus at Christmas time, we knew all too well that Christmas pointed us to the sadness, depth of despair, and cruelty of a hill far away on a Friday, for some reason called Good. And now in great contrast that moment of harsh awakening has arrived. That mountain of fantasy and of angelic song have been transformed into a hill that tells us of the utmost devastation of feeling forsaken by you, even his Father. Instead of a babe in a manger, there is a cross, supreme, sacrificial pain and suffering, death as the wages of sin, not his own.

Temper, we pray, the heart rending sadness and mourning of this horrible Friday with the anticipation of the joy of Easter and with expectations unheard of-the gifts of redemption, salvation, and the mysteries beyond, even life eternal, extended also to a repentant criminal, who died right there with Jesus Christ.

And as we find ourselves in the valley at the tomb, as we have many times stood at the open graves of loved ones and of friends, we thank you that seed does not germinate and flourish in new life, unless it first seems to die, falls to the earth, and is buried.

Thanks be to you for that hill, for redemption, for salvation, and for the hope of life eternal, throbbing in our hearts, so dearly and so painfully bought.

Daniel J. Theron

Thanks be to you that now we can know why that sad Friday of the old rugged cross of shame, suffering, and pain, for our sake, can be called "Good Friday." ....Amen.

Easter Sunday

Thanks be to you, O Lord, the strife is over, the battle won. The ugly grave has become but a memory of transformation. The hill of suffering and shame has once more been transfigured into a mountain of rejoicing and singing. Thanks be to you that the joy and message of Christmas have now come full circle and to full fruition in a loud Hallelujah of life eternal!

We thank you for a life that had fulfilled faithfully what you had purposed it to do, even sacrificing itself vicariously with suffering for the salvation of sinful people, to bring a message of redemption of the world.

We thank you that the message of Easter goes out to all the earth.

We thank you that the triumph over the futility of life has been won for us forever.

We thank you that the power of sin has been conquered and that its wages have been paid.

We thank you that in faith and hope we can see through the sting, and threat, and darkness of death to envision eternity, and that in hope we can now celebrate the victory of life eternal as our heritage.

We thank you that peace on earth, which we so cherished at Christmas time, can now become a reality.

We thank you that your Kingdom on earth was so made more real as coming into our midst.

44

Hear Our Prayers And Hymns, O Lord, We Pray

Thanks be to you, Almighty God, our Father, Holy Spirit, to whom with Jesus Christ be all glory, all honor, and all praise for ever and ever. Hallelujah and Amen!

Life Eternal

O Lord, our God, we stand in awe of the inexorable laws that govern your creation, that set boundaries to the span of human existence on earth. You have instituted time and you have extended it to eternity. As our Father, you have made us part of both time and eternity. We thank you for the seed, the awareness, and the yearning of eternal life implanted and throbbing in every heart. Teach us so to consider our sojourn in time on this earth that we shall apply our hearts to wisdom, and that we shall so fashion our lives as to be worthy of eternity....Amen.

Prosperity

Save us dear Lord, from corruption that comes with ease; save us from obliviousness of the pain and suffering of our fellow human beings that comes from isolation in luxury; and above all, save us from forgetfulness of you that comes with continuous prosperity.

Render us grateful, that thankful hearts may save us from these follies. Grant, we pray, that we, with all that you have bestowed upon us so liberally, shall be worthy and useful in your Kingdom on earth.
....Amen.

Daniel J. Theron

Talents and Crosses

Almighty God, our Father, we thank you that to all of us you have given talents. Be there five, or be there two, or be there only one, enable us so fully to use our talents that all may benefit.

And to some of us you have given a cross to bear, physical or mental handicaps, illness, or sorrow. Be that cross heavy, or be it light, make us willing to bear one end of it that every cross may indeed be light....Amen.

Our Privilege in God's World

Almighty God, you have created around us a universe and a world of means so unmeasured and of power so unlimited as to be completely beyond our comprehension. In your goodness you have granted the human race the ability to unlock some of the mysteries of your creation, and you have empowered us to use the endless resources of power, hidden in your handiwork, planet earth, which is our home. We are grateful to you that with these powers we may supply, even more than sufficient, in all our needs and comforts. Grant mankind the wisdom, we pray, that it shall use these powers so discovered, not foolishly for destruction, but wisely for building up a world of peace, sharing in love and brotherhood with others living under the burden of misfortune.

For what we so richly enjoy of your bounty, this day and all the days of our lives, we come humbly, and we give thanks....Amen.

Almighty God, our Father, we thank you that your fatherhood extends to all people: to the brilliant as well as to the mentally and physically disadvantaged; to beautiful people as well as to the unattractive; to the well groomed as well as to the tramp; to the good citizen as well as to the criminal; to our friends, as well as to our enemies.

Keep us humble, we pray, knowing that we are nothing and have nothing that we have not received, and that, but for the gift of your grace, we would be the lowly tramp, the criminal, and enemies, even your enemies.

In humility may we see ourselves as we truly are, we pray....Amen.

Humor

Our Father, creator of all, we marvel that in the wonders of your universe you did not neglect to display a sense of humor, in creating the unbelievable camel with a hump and sometimes two, and a trot hard to believe, in endowing the donkey with his heart-rending bray, and the crow with its ear-piercing squawk, and even the skunk with its surprise.

We thank you that while there is a time to weep, there is also a time to laugh. We give thanks for human beings endowed with a sense of humor to lighten our burdens of life and to teach us that there is a time to relax with laughter; for the humorists who can bring a smile to our faces with their words; for those who can invent wholesome jokes to help us ease tensions and to further fellowship; for the cartoonist who can see humor in so many situations of life and can make us see ourselves, and induce us to laugh even at ourselves, and also to gain wisdom.

For our own good, grant us an eye and an ear for what is funny, and also the ability to laugh often, we pray....Amen.

Sport

Dear Lord, we thank you that we can so conduct our lives as to be healthy, strong, filled with joy, and happiness; we thank you for the development of many forms of sport; for skis and skates that slide; for balls that bounce and fly; for clubs and bats and rackets; all sorts of things that we can throw, or kick, or swing; for the fellowship and exercise that all these bring; for fun, healthy appetites that follow, and good digestion, but above all also for plenty to digest....Amen.

MAY

Mother's Day

God, our Father, we thank you for the all surpassing gift that you have bestowed upon mankind-your matchless love for us as your children.

And on Mother's Day, especially, we thank you for the manifestation of that love in the lives of our mothers. We thank you for their devotion to those whom you have entrusted to them as their children; for their continuous concern and abiding love with which they watch over them, sacrifice, and provide for them; for their unselfish devotion to them, sometimes undeserved; for many prayers of intercession, sometimes with tears, on behalf of their children throughout all of their lives.

As we commend our mothers to you, we especially remember so many mothers on whose shoulders rests the great responsibility of single parenthood, whatever the cause may be. In their difficult task be their unseen companion, their comfort, and their strength.

Grant that the presence of mothers among us this day, and the memories of those already departed to the life beyond, will be constant reminders of how much they mean to all of us and to all the world.

May they also point us to your unfailing love, to your care, and to your goodness toward us, all the days of our lives....Amen.

Nature and Stewardship

Almighty God, our Father, as springtime awakens and bursts out around us, we come to you as the master artist. We thank you for the world decked in splendor- a planet which you have given us as our home, sweet home, for valleys carpeted in green, for singing streams, for endless, undulating plains, for majestic mountains, sentinels telling us that our Watchman never slumbers, nor sleeps; for the marvels of trees and flowers that sprout at their appointed time; for butterflies and birds, and for all beautiful things that on your good earth do dwell.

Grant that we shall hold the beauty of the earth as a sacred trust from you, because you have made it so pristine; that we shall seek to preserve the grandeur of the work of your hands for all generations to come;

Hear Our Prayers And Hymns, O Lord, We Pray
that we shall be worthy stewards of all creatures, great and small, even of plants that make earth their home, for they also are part of your creation; that we shall cultivate love and respect for our fellow human beings, because they have been made in your image.
....Amen.

Attitude of Service

Almighty God, our Father, we thank you for the multitude of responsibilities and opportunities of service in places of worship where the presence of your Kingdom on earth can be made so real to us.

Grant that we shall be willing to do small things when you call us to do small things, and that we may be found worthy when you summon us to daunting and loftier duties.

Lord, we often get lost in the maze of life. We deem ourselves virtuous for upholding laws made by human beings. Instead, bestow upon us, we pray, a deep awareness of our own need of redemption and personal commitment to what you have revealed to us through many centuries as our personal faith and rule of life.

When we are favored, grant us the gift of gratitude and humility; when we are wronged, give us the grace to forgive.

When we prosper, endow us with a spirit of nobleness, gratitude, and generosity; when we are thwarted and frustrated, enable us to be long-suffering, courageous, and seeking, but at all times striving to do your will, we pray....Amen.

Daniel J. Theron

Kentucky Derby

Almighty God, for Springtime around us in all its
beauty and splendor,
For renewal of nature and spirit from shore to shore,
For a time to gather for frolic and Kentucky Derby
fun,
For preparation and exercise until so special a race
is won,
For the beauty of the prancing and spirited steed,
For daring jockeys and horses' amazing speed,
For the passing of "The Old Kentucky Home" and the day
of the slave,
For freedom wherever the Star-spangled Banner may
wave,
For the challenge of life's race in which we all run,
-The race which we all want to win-
   For happiness, fellowship, and abundance in which
we share,
Lord, giver of all, to you with thanksgiving, we lift
today this our prayer!...Amen.

Fellowship

   Our Father, we thank you for the host of witnesses
who have gone before us; for believers invisible,
present and past; for your Kingdom on earth and for
your Kingdom beyond; for your calling, graciously
extended to us to be part of that fellowship of the
faithful, and part of that Kingdom, here and now and
yet coming.
   Having been thus favored, grant that your presence
and inspiration shall so strongly well up in us that

52

we may become powerful witnesses in what we speak and do, not only to build up the fellowship of believers, but especially to bring the presence of your Kingdom into the hearts of human beings, and so into this dark and floundering world around us. Hear our prayer, O Lord, we pray....Amen.

Pentecost/Whitsunday

1

Lord, our God, we stand in awe of the mystery of the universe around us, in awe of the mystery of the world of which we are a part, and in awe of your silent presence at work in all of it, because you are Spirit. We stand in awe of the mystery and power imparted to us because you as Spirit dwell in us, and make your presence more real to us.

We thank you for your spiritual power that inspired prophets, priests, apostles, evangelists, and godly people throughout the centuries; for your voice that they heard and the message that they proclaimed throughout world history to mankind, establishing your laws and making known your will on earth; for sacred Scriptures of the ages handed down and preserving your guide lines and rules of faith and life for us-a lamp unto our feet.

We thank you that you as mysterious Spirit brought us to life in this world and dwell in us. As we struggle against our proneness to evil, grant that your godliness may so well up in us as to remind us of your laws and your will that striving for holiness may pervade our coming and our going, and that we may overcome evil, and triumph in the end, redeemed as full citizens of your Kingdom.

We thank you for the spiritual guidance in our own lives in so many ways, if we would but listen-in sacred writings bequeathed to us, in godly people around us, and in the small voice of our own inner self. Enable us, we pray, to be attuned to such guidance that we may courageously face the world in which it is too easy to go astray.

And when the sun is beginning to touch the horizon, the shadows of life are growing longer, and our earthly tabernacle is about to be folded, grant that triumph, victory, and hope of life everlasting shall rise like a newborn sun. Grant then, O Lord, Eternal Spirit, that you may so possess us as to make real in us that yearning for life eternal that throbs in every human heart. So changed to glory take us in joy to our eternal home where there are many mansions.
....Amen.

2

Almighty God, our Father, as we celebrate Pentecost, we thank you that we are once again on a high mountain in the life of your Church.

We confess that this day is often neglected and forgotten. We thank you for those, even in our time, who gather ten days in meetings for prayer to prepare themselves and to wait eagerly for a fuller awareness on this festive day of your presence in their hearts as Holy Spirit.

Grant us the patience with great expectation to wait like the disciples of old, so as to be adequately

equipped before launching out to do your bidding in
the world.

We thank you, as mysterious as it may seem to us,
that, nevertheless, you dwell in us as Spirit so that,
by your grace, we may be inspired, if we would only
wait and anticipate patiently.

We thank you for the beginning of your Church at
the time of Pentecost to be a haven of comfort, a
communion of fellowship, a source of power in the
lives of your people, and an instrument of your
Kingdom in all the world; for the miraculous growth of
the Church empowered by your Holy Presence through
the centuries; for that power that continues to
inspire your Church and its witnesses to bring the
message of redemption, of salvation, and of your
Kingdom with all its glory and benefits to the
uttermost ends of the earth; for the power enabling
us, not only to do what is difficult, but even to
fulfill impossible dreams.

We thank you for the abiding fellowship of your
indwelling in us that aids us to get a glimpse of the
marvels of your hand in the universe around us, that
reveals to us the mystery of your ways with mankind
such as we can comprehend, that makes your nearness
more real to us, that comforts us, reveals the truth
to us, leads us in your righteousness, and equips us
for the task of each day.

On this day of Pentecost empty our hearts of what
is worldly and unworthy. Cause, we pray, that your
presence in us will well up with such great strength
that, in some small way, we may be your power wherever
we would find ourselves in the world.

55

Daniel J. Theron

To you, our God, Holy Spirit, and to Christ be all honor, all glory, and all praise, always....Amen.

Memorial Day /Soldiers' Day

1

Almighty God, our Father, out of one blood you have created all peoples on the earth, and in your hands are the destinies of all nations. As we commemorate Memorial Day, we confess that our race goes to war because evil in our hearts gains the upper hand over good, greed vanquishes contentment, and humility succumbs to pride.

Where we have fought side by side for justice and for the quest of liberty, we thank you for might and for victory. Where we have gone to battle to satisfy our greed, we ask for forgiveness and for such magnanimity as to more than heal the wounds of those who should have been our brothers and our sisters, but whom we have made our enemies, and whom we have wronged. Enable us to make more than full restitution.

On this day we shed a tear as we honor those for whom the sun had set while it was still day, who did not return from their missions, and who never came home. May we hold in sacred and loving memory their selflessness, their bravery, and their devotion to offer themselves to country and to principle to the very end of their lives.

As we honor those who have been sacrificed in war and on battle fields, grant, O Lord, above all that we shall be soldiers in the mighty array of your eternal Kingdom, that we shall prevail and be victorious, not against flesh and blood, but against the powers of darkness that lurk within ourselves that bring strife, war, bloodshed, and tears upon our world.

So may your Kingdom come on earth, not by might, nor by power, but by your Spirit in brotherhood and peace on earth....Amen.

2

Almighty God, our Father, once again it is Memorial Day. We cannot but confess the folly of mankind that made necessary this commemoration:

Mankind's folly has made the taking of lives a virtue.

By our folly millions through the ages have perished violently in battle and were wasted.

By the same folly millions of innocent victims have perished, millions have been left homeless, widowed, and orphaned.

In hatred we have destroyed what has taken generations to build up. We have brought home the decadence of war that infects our societies and that lowers our morality.

We confess that we have failed to learn that your way is not by might, guns, bombs, or by the power of the sword, but by the silent and most powerful way- your Spirit.

In your great mercy grant that mankind's repentance for the death of those who have perished in the violence of war, will hasten the day when missiles of destruction will be turned into vehicles of transportation or other instruments of peace; when the energy and marvels of your creation will no longer be fashioned into instruments of devastation, but will be harnessed only for the service, comfort, and progress

57

of mankind; when the law of your Kingdom, the law of love, and not the law of evil hearts, will be the law of the world in brotherhood, in peace, in harmony, and in tranquility....Amen.

3

Almighty God, our Father, who has made mankind to be one family, we confess before you our shortcomings that made this day of solemn commemoration a necessity.

We confess the greed, lust for power, lack of compassion and lack of understanding that made for the horrors of war, bloodshed, tears, and the death of many, mostly in the morning of their lives.

So touch the heart of humanity with the supreme sacrifices of those whom we here remember and honor today, we pray, that they shall not have died in vain, but shall have been sacrificed to redeem us from the scourge of warfare....Amen.

4

Almighty God, our Father, as we celebrate this day of heroes, we bring homage to, and we thank you for those in ages past who have made the ultimate sacrifice, the sacrifice of life itself, on battlefields across this globe, those who, in spite of harm's way, lived by the motto that "It is sweet and fitting to die for one's fatherland."

We thank you for the struggles for liberty and justice.

Nevertheless, we confess the evil of violence and aggrandizement in war; taking by might what you have bequeathed to another.

Hear Our Prayers And Hymns, O Lord, We Pray

Guide us to a superior way, the way which is not by aggrandizement, might, power, war, bloodshed, death, destruction, and suffering, but by your Spirit. Show and lead us in the way to brotherhood, civility, love, and peace-the way of the laws of your Kingdom, we pray....Amen.

JUNE

The Truth

O God, our Father, we thank you for the rule of truth that governs your creation and should also govern our own lives, if we would only open our minds and our hearts to it. Grant, we pray, that truth will be our guide in researching and understanding your revelation as it has been made known to us in writings through the centuries and in other ways around us, and especially as we attempt to reduce it all to creeds and confessions. Grant that we shall not close our minds to revelation as it comes to us in scientific research, but that with gratitude we shall have the wisdom to combine it all as sacred revelation from you to form a bulwark of truth in your service in the world as we progress through history. Liberate us from the folly of insecurity that goes to great lengths and waste of time in attempting to prove what is untenable in the court of truth, and although with good intentions, mislead those entrusted to us. Grant us the courage to abandon without struggle, but with gladness, what we have for so long regarded as unquestionably true, but which the judge of truth rejects. We thank you for the power of hope and imagination with which Christianity has inspired generations through the ages as a foundation of creativity and art in our civilization. As we continue to hold dear what is legendary, imagination, and symbolic, grant us the keenness to find within these the kernels of truth so often obscured, and to nurture those kernels of truth until they wax to full maturity and fruition, nourishing and inspiring our spirits, our minds, and our reason, and the world around us.

So render us strong ambassadors of the truth to bring your greatness to your people, that we may as one serve you with pride, with gladness, and above all without strife, we pray....Amen.

The Choice of Wisdom

O Lord, teach us not to rush in when we should pray;

Not to pray when we should act;

Not to meditate when we should speak;

Not to speak when silence would be golden.

Grant us the wisdom, we pray, when and which to choose....Amen.

Grace at a Wedding Reception

O God, our Father, we come to you with thanksgiving in our hearts for our friends [Debra and Ronald] who, in your providence, have found each other, and who this day have publicly set the seal of vows upon their love for each other. We thank you that our hearts can rejoice with them in celebrating and witnessing this meaningful and memorable day of their marriage and their happiness.

In your great goodness enable them to cradle with care, through the bumps and knocks of life, the fragile treasure of love which you have bestowed upon them to have and to hold as a trust. As they journey

61

together, grant them at all times the treasures of mutual respect and confidence in one another that their love for one another may grow strong and indestructible. Bestow upon them your grace, your benediction, and a full measure of sunshine throughout life, we pray.

We thank you for the opportunity of merrymaking and for the abundance in which we share. We would acknowledge that you have given us so much more than our daily bread. For all these, in one accord with those who have found each other in love, we come to you with the gratitude of our hearts....Amen.

Graduation/Commencement

1

Almighty God, our Father, while millions of our contemporaries, the world over, are unable even to read, or to write, or to calculate, we thank you for the favor bestowed on this generation to pursue learning far beyond elementary schooling.

We are thankful that today we can honor the graduates of this institution [name], who have gathered here to be acknowledged and to receive their rewards for arduous years of study and accumulation of knowledge and skills.

We are grateful for parents and others who enabled them financially-sometimes at great sacrifice-to attend an institution of learning; for those-many no longer with us-who have contributed to endowments or created foundations for scholarships; for those graduating who were able to help themselves with the work of their own hands and minds.

Hear Our Prayers And Hymns, O Lord, We Pray

We are grateful for those among us whose calling in life is teaching. For their dedication to research and expansion of their own knowledge that they may enrich the minds of generations to come, the least of which is not those who are graduating here today.

We commend to you those whose lives are quietly dedicated to the administration of this institution, the President and all who devote their lives to its excellence.

We shall be remiss if not remembering all those-often not seen and unknown to us-who labor with their hands to serve this institution.

For the privilege granted those who are about to graduate to have gathered knowledge, to have broadened their horizons of life, to have learned independence of thinking, to have set goals, and to have challenged the status quo, we give thanks to you.

Above all may they depart from this institution with the sure conviction and comfort that the beginning of all wisdom is the fear of the Lord.

So bless them, we pray, as they journey through life. And to your great name be glory, praise, and thanksgiving....Amen.

2

Lord, our God, who has made studying and the gathering of knowledge possible for those who this day will receive their rewards, impress upon them that this exercise is not an end, but indeed a new beginning. As they now launch out into the unknown, be it for higher degrees, or new employment, grant that together with the knowledge and skills that they have

The Beginning of Wisdom is the fear of the Lord

absorbed and acquired during their years of hard work, there shall also rise within them the muscle of moral fiber and a fountain of wisdom; that they shall not regard the definition of the source of wisdom as old fashioned, out of date, or an old cliché-because it is tested. Therefore, enable them, and teach us all anew, we pray, to live by the proven motto that the beginning of wisdom is the fear of the Lord.

We pray not that their careers, soon to be commenced, shall be easy, but we do pray that they shall be filled with inspiration not to shy away from daunting challenges, mustering their abilities and their courage to persevere to the top of ever higher peaks and new, distant vistas in their lives. Grant them the strength to face adversity boldly and to overcome each challenge in their lives that in the end they may be victors who have attained their destinations and goals, worthy of the commendation: "Well done, well done!"

And now to your great name, fountain of knowledge, and of wisdom, and of strength, be glory, and praise, and thanksgiving, always....Amen.

Grace at a Meal

1

O God, our Father, we always know too well and we complain when it is too hot, or when it is too cold; when it rains too much, or when there is a drought; when the wind blows too much, or when it snows too much. Nevertheless, for the heat of the summer, for the cold of winter that plant and earth may rest, for times when it rains or snows, for the wind that blows, and for the sun that may be hot-all that the earth may bring forth abundantly to provide in our needs, especially the food prepared for us-we come to you, and we give thanks....Amen.

2

Our Father, we rejoice in the favor of yet another day.

We thank you for yet another meal.

Bless both this day and this food to our bodies and to our minds to serve you better with whatever talents we have been endowed.

And remember all our loved ones, we pray....Amen.

3

Almighty God, our Father, our prayer is often for daily bread. But in your great goodness to us you have given us so much more than our daily bread. We pause to give thanks for so much in life that we enjoy. And now for the food of which we are about to partake and for our fellowship as we are gathered together, we humble ourselves, and we give thanks....Amen.

4

Almighty God, our Father, we thank you that you as our host set a table before us under all circumstances and in all conditions of life: a table of consolation and comfort when we are in sorrow, mourning, and adversity; a table of rejoicing in times of joy and gladness. And so many times the cup that you set before us runs over. We thank you that today you have prepared for us, your people, a table of fellowship. Receive our thanks for the food of which we are about to partake. As you have blessed us abundantly, enable us to pass on to others a portion of fellowship and joy, which we here share together, we pray....Amen.

5

God, our Father, we remember so many who have less than we do.

We remember so many in stress of floods, winds, and storms.

Nevertheless, we thank you for the rain that falls, for snow that covers the earth that it may rest for the winter, for the winds that blow, for the sun that shines, all working together that the earth may bring forth abundantly to supply in so much of our needs.

Bless us as we enjoy a meal together, and make us a blessing to others, we pray....Amen.

6

Bless this food , O Lord, to our bodies that we may be effective to the best of our abilities in our assigned task of life, especially in the service of your Kingdom, we pray....Amen.

A Cross to Bear

Lord, we thank you for those among us who silently and courageously, walk, or struggle in the shadow of a daily cross, even with a smile on their faces, because you are bearing one end of that cross. And we thank you for many who in your name are willing to help others to carry their burden of a cross on their shoulders....Amen.

Flag Day

Almighty God, our Father, we thank you for many banners that freely over us wave; for the inspiration with which the flag has spurred on, and still is spurring on the courageous and the brave, even to lay down their lives for it; for being the symbol of patriotism, the symbol of loyalty to our constitution and the laws derived from it; for being the symbol of pride in a land of industry and splendor from boundary to boundary.

As we are grateful for our flag, may it point us to a banner, so much higher, and so much superior, that waves over our world so often in utter turmoil, the banner of your Kingdom, summoning us with the exhortation: "Excelsior, excelsior!"...Amen.

Morning

For the morning star, harbinger of a new day,
For light that drives the dark away,
For birds jubilant in the trees,
For the refreshing of the morning breeze,
Lord, ruler and giver of all, to you we offer
Praise and thanksgiving with this our morning
prayer....Amen.

Noon

For the sun, ruler of our sky,
For clouds like castles drifting by,
For rain that plants and flowers may grow,
That streams may gurgle and rivers may flow,
Lord, ruler and giver of all, to you we offer,
Praise and thanksgiving with this our noontime
prayer...Amen.

For the farewell rays of the sun
When the toil of the day is done,
For another day to have labored and tried our best,
For the evening star that now calls us to rest,
Lord, ruler and giver of all, to you we offer,
Praise and thanksgiving with this our evening
prayer....Amen.

Evening

Daniel J. Theron

Father's Day

Almighty God, as we think of your fatherhood, we know all too well that we are not perfect fathers. But we do love our children, although we are not so good putting our love into practice on a daily basis. Yet, when the chips are down, we will stand up for them, we promise.

We usually provide for our children, but so often, instead of love, we give them too much of things that really do not count. We spoil them.

We confess that often we fail to see the shortcomings of our own children, and when we do, grant that we shall not be at a loss about effective discipline or counseling-not too much, and not too little.

We are so aware of the all-important daily newspaper when a son needs us to jump up and down with him around the basketball hoop, or kick a ball back and forth, or pitch a baseball to his feeble bat. And our pitching is usually not that good anyway.

Grant that we shall not feel so sorry for ourselves for having lived through a bad day at the office that we are deaf to the urgent pleas of a sweet little girl: "Daddy, come and hold my bike and run beside me to teach me how to ride." And how would she ever learn, if I do not run by her side? Why did we give her the bike to begin with?

In the pressure of life we have such short memories about birthdays and other dates so important to our children. Grant us the ability to make knots in our memories!

We take for granted the accomplishments of our children and can easily be sparing with praise and a big hug that are of so much more value to them than money, or material things.

We admit to the big sigh of relief when the nest is finally empty and blaring rock music is replaced by divine silence, when other, annoying habits no longer irk us, when they are at last out from under our feet. Yet, we still treat them as "little girl" and "little boy." Help us to grow up too and to let go when we have to.

Lord, we would be perfect fathers like you. Come to the aid of our imperfection, we pray....Amen.

Our Children

Almighty God, Father of mankind, you entrust to each generation, and so to us, the heavy responsibility of its youth, its children, and its grandchildren. You have laid upon our shoulders the burden of brining up those who will be the adults of tomorrow, the citizens, the fathers and the mothers, the leaders of the generation to come. Enable us to shoulder this our task and burden with the needed sacrifice, dignity, wisdom, and joy.

As we live in our era of great advantages of science and technology that can bring plenty to all, we lament that many children, the world over, still live under dismal conditions of want and ignorance. Above all do we lament the abuse and the leading astray of the innocent, even in our own midst. Enable us not to stand by idly.

71

So we commend the youth of our day to your care. Enable us to provide in their needs, be they spiritual or material, we pray. Guide them patiently through the long and arduous toil of education, through the dangers of growing up that will beset them on all sides. Make not their way easy, but grant them the strength to triumph over temptation, iniquity, and evil, that in the end they may be stronger for having fought the good fight and emerge as victors. As we commend our young people, our children, and our grandchildren to your care, grant us to know that our care is above all also your care entrusted to us.

And when time brings our youth to the age when the desire of independence knocks at the door, grant that we shall so have acquitted ourselves of the tasks assigned to us, that they shall be able to stand alone, make wise choices, weather the wind, the rain, and the storms of life, in the end to enjoy the sunshine destined for them.

Enable us, we ask, always to share with new generations, their enthusiasm, their daring, their dreams, and their great expectations that are the foundations of tomorrow.

Bind us together as families, as communities, and as nations in a common concern for new generations coming into this world, for in them you have committed to us the future.

Grant that we shall joyfully accept the challenges and responsibilities that come with parenthood....Amen.

Hear Our Prayers And Hymns, O Lord, We Pray
Conquering Diseases

Almighty God, we thank you for the task of having dominion over much of the earth that you have graciously entrusted to us as human beings. We thank you especially for those whose task in life has been, and still is, dedication to research and the ministry of medicine that we may enjoy healthier bodies and happier lives. We thank you for the measure of success with which you have rewarded their labors-for making us more aware of balanced diets and exercise; for preventing disease with vaccines, especially the crippling disease of polio, and even eradicating the scourge of smallpox from the earth; for giant pharmaceutical companies that spend decades in research to find and produce wonder drugs that alleviate suffering, cure so many ailments, and prolong our lives; for the refinement of surgery beyond our imagination to correct, replace, and heal even essential structures of our bodies.

We commend to your care those still suffering from maladies for which there is yet no cure-cancer, multiple sclerosis, Parkinson's, Alzheimer's, and many other diseases. Grant success to those who dedicate their lives in the continuous battle against these and all other afflictions that still ravage mankind, we pray....Amen.

JULY

Making and Taking Time to. . . :

1

Lord, we thank you that you have placed each one of us on this earth as a member of the human race with a purpose. But we confess that sometimes our grasp of these purposes are so vague that we wander around aimlessly. At other times, we must confess, that we are so obsessed with our own purposes that we rush headlong to catch a bus, a plane, or meet an appointment on time with utter disregard for order and common sense in arranging and wisely conducting our lives.

Teach us, we earnestly pray, even during the busiest of days to make such time and to take such time as needed:

To establish daily communion with you, our maker, from whom came our spirits, that we may be inspired, lifted up, and refreshed to face each day confidently, courageously, and boldly;

To meditate and contemplate on things unseen and eternal that we may gain a deeper and better knowledge of you, ourselves, our fellow human beings, and our calling in life;

To do our best to live more harmonious and prolonged lives in fulfilling more adequately both the great and the small purposes assigned to each one of us during our sojourn on this earth....Amen.

Teach us, O Lord, we pray, so to consider those who live with us on this earth that we shall take time and make time:

To build friendships with a smile, a compliment, a word of appreciation, or encouragement that we may strengthen the warp and woof of the fabric that holds humanity together;

To build relationships and maintain family kinships across the world with the marvels of communications at our finger tips, a letter, a long distance telephone call, an e-mail, to remove the barriers that destroy the bonds of unity binding us all together as your family;

To intersperse both our labor and our leisure with a sense of humor to provide relaxation and the spice of life;

To practise patience and patience again and again that can shoulder such heavy burdens, even under trying conditions, for the furthering of good will and understanding;

To work hard at turning the growl into a smile;

To reign in temper with self-control and to use sweetness rather than a sting;

To still troubled waters that there may be harmony and peace;

To give rather than to receive, for it is in giving that we become rich in what really counts;

To be honest, for the truth will sooner or later catch up with the lie. And you know it all anyway from the very beginning;

To so order our conduct with our fellow human beings that our lives, at least in some small way, will be a ministry to them in your name....Amen.

3

Lord, as life so often hurtles along at high speed, enable us to force upon ourselves moments of introspection and meditation, enabling us to take time and to make time:

To savor the broad smile of a thousand sunrises on our sojourn through life as they joyously embrace our world in the morning with their arms of gold, inspiring our hearts with a new song to enjoy our privileges, and courageously to meet the challenges of yet another day;

Never to stop mingling facts with dreams of vision, and to build castles;

Nevertheless, to burn our candles only at one end, for doing it otherwise, at both ends, will eventually be a waste;

To avoid excesses in all of life, for in the end they will destroy;

To have fun and frolic and recreation that we may benefit from the ancient secret that a vibrant spirit and a clear mind can live and serve much better in a sound body;

To be good people with great hearts, open in love to our fellow human beings, and even to all creatures and plants that inhabit the earth with us;

To undergird the burdens that we must bear with the mighty pillars of humor and laughter;

To read every day something wholesome and edifying bequeathed to us by those in times past, who by your grace have been wise that we also may gain wisdom and come to terms with the world and life around us;

To treat our ears and spirits every day to a little good music that it may bring peace to our troubled hearts and that it may transport us into realms unknown to so many of us;

To study works of art that we may view the marvels of creation through the eyes of those whom you have endowed with special, creative gifts to be artists, and so to broaden our own minds and vision of your world....Amen.

4

And when the day is done, grant that we shall take time:

To savor the peaceful splendor of a thousand sunsets in wings of scarlet and gold embracing our own small world; that we shall make time to marvel at the dazzling farewell of colored banners so masterfully painted in the canopy of clouds, shortly to be furled into the cover of peace and rest of night;

To gaze at the heavens in astonishment and utter amazement as the spacious universe envelopes us with its billions of lamps across the firmament all over and around, that we may come to grasp with how small and insignificant we indeed are, and how truly great and merciful you are, even to us;

To welcome with gladness the shadows of eventide as they advance over our surroundings, pull a blanket over us and whisper in our ears: "Sufficient unto this day have now been both the good and the evil thereof. Bury your worry in the satisfaction that this day you have done your duty. You must now cease from your labors. Benefit from the fruit of those labors. Rest and sleep in peace and confidence and soundness as your Creator has intended for you to enjoy, for your watchman never sleeps, nor slumbers;"

So to order the purposes of our lives that once we must lay down our heads for the last time, some of what we have planned and cherish to accomplish during our life spans will still be left unfinished to be committed into your hands to inspire those who follow us in life.

Above all, Lord, enable us to make time and to take time, whenever possible, even more than within our limited power lies, to heed the greatest of all your commandments: "Be holy, for I am holy."...Amen.

On the Road, in the Air, on the Water

O God, you are the source of all power. In your goodness you have endowed the inquisitive with the capacity to unlock the powers that you have hidden in and around us in this world. We thank you for probing minds through the centuries that have discovered these powers and have harnessed them for our use, especially for quick and convenient transportation, be it on land, or sea, or in the air.

We commend to your care the millions who this day and every day take to the road, sail, or fly.

We commend to you those entrusted with the safety of roads and well functioning of our travel equipment; those who have in their hands the lives of thousands of travelers-the engineer, the driver, the pilot, and the captain; those who manage and control traffic-the dispatcher, the policeman, the air traffic controller, the light house attendant, and many others.

Protect, we pray, and grant wisdom especially to our young people who feel the exhilaration of a wheel in their hands, wheels under them, and the vroom, vroom of power under the hood, more than human beings need, and often can not handle.

Grant that the privilege and ease of traveling long distances in a short time shall be enjoyed for the pleasure and benefit of all without needless tragedies, undue loss of life and limb....Amen.

Independence Day

1

Almighty God, ruler of all nations, as we commemorate our natal day, the birth of the country to which we pledge allegiance, we thank you that in your great providence a new nation was brought forth on these shores.

We thank you that even as you have ordained spring and summer to break the bondage of a bitter winter at Valley Forge, so at your appointed time, was liberty won and independence established.

Through the circling years you have been our refuge and our strength. You have blessed us far beyond our expectations, and far beyond our deserving to dwell from ocean to ocean in the midst of plenty and in the splendor of your handiwork.

Our tables are laden from day to day with more than what is sufficient. Truly, our cup runs over.

Grant, O Lord, that our enjoyment of abundance and of liberty will be exceeded only by our own sense of responsibility; that, for the benefit of all peoples, we may go forward as one nation under you, indivisible, despite our great diversity, with liberty, love, and justice for all; that we may be to the world a beacon of hope and light, set on a hill, that cannot be hid.

And to your great name be all honor, and praise, and thanksgiving for freedom and abundance that we enjoy....Amen.

2

As we celebrate Independence Day, we thank you for the beauty of the land in which we live.

We are especially grateful for the wisdom and greatness embodied in our Constitution, the foundation of our government and the guarantee of our liberty and freedom.

We would also thank you for the wisdom of freedom of expression that is guaranteed. Grant, we pray, as we enjoy this freedom, that we shall also demand and exercise responsibility in speaking the truth, in rendering respect for the flag of our country, in observing the excellence of decency, in appreciating true beauty and decorum, be it in what we say, or be it in what we produce as art. In whatever medium we employ to express ourselves, may we always be guided by your revelation and your wisdom made manifest to mankind through many centuries to serve as the foundation and rule of divine faith and life.

Grant that the interpretation of our Constitution, which we claim as the final protection for our lives and liberties, shall be done equally with grave responsibility, rooted in wisdom emanating from your guidance as accumulated through the circling years.

And now to you, Great Father of all, we entrust for the centuries to come this our dear land of liberty, of beauty, and of splendor....Amen.

3

Almighty God, in whose hand are the birth and the destinies of nations, we thank you for the day that brought liberty to this land.

We thank you for the influence of religion and education, the foundations of civility and decency so that the tradition of democracy and self-rule can survive and thrive through many centuries to come.

Grant that the torch of freedom will shine brightly not only over us as a light of hope in the midst of gloom, of ignorance, and of inhumanity of man to man, but that it shall also be a rallying beacon to all the world.

Make us worthy of the gift of freedom which you have entrusted to us that we may not only preserve it for ourselves, but also pass it's torch on to others, we pray....Amen.

4

Almighty God, our Father, as we celebrate our day of independence, we give thanks for our flag of liberty that freely over us waves in many places.

As we from day to day so richly enjoy our freedom and the pursuit of happiness, so often depending on the things that money can buy, grant that we shall never be oblivious of our superior motto, In God we Trust, stamped on billions of our coins, and daily passing through millions of hands mostly unnoticed, for without dependence on you and trust in you, for without the great power that you have entrusted to mankind, for without love in our hearts that comes from you, we will avail nothing worthwhile and lasting.

In you do we indeed put our trust....Amen.

Receiving, Giving, and Serving

Almighty God, our heavenly Father, often we are in your presence to speak, rather than to listen; to receive rather than to plan how we can give. In life we so often want help where we can help ourselves; we wish to be ministered unto, rather than to minister.

Enable us, we pray, so to order our lives and our priorities that we may more frequently listen to your still, small voice within us, and more often give of ourselves and of our substance.

Whether we speak or listen, whether we receive or give, enable us to minister to others, but above all to serve you with our whole heart, mind, soul, and with all our strength....Amen.

Grace at a Meal

We sing your mighty power, O Lord, that made majestic mountains rise, that carved out fertile valleys that grain may grow, that stretched out endless plains that sheep and cattle may roam, that so wonderfully and so generously supplies in all our needs, especially the sustenance of our bodies here

Hear Our Prayers And Hymns, O Lord, We Pray
prepared for us. Before you we humble ourselves and we
give thanks....Amen.

The Presence of God in All Things

Almighty God, Creator of all that encompasses us,
we stand in awe of the mystery, the beauty, and the
wonder with which you have made the universe in which
we are privileged to live and of which we are a part.

We thank you for the human mind that can, like
children, explore and try to unravel what you have so
intricately put together. We are grateful that we can
be part of the electronic age, the nuclear age, the
space age, the age of wonder drugs, and the age of
genetic engineering with all the comforts that we
enjoy in our time. Grant us the wisdom, we ask, that
we will shoulder the unspeakable challenges and
responsibilities that come with the knowledge and the
new abilities entrusted to us.

We thank you that your presence is near to us in
all conditions of life, not only on the mountain tops
of great discoveries and accomplishments, but also in
the small things of life, the drop of water, the lump
of clay, the plant and flower by the wayside. Grant
that your presence will be even more real in the
valley of every day living, in the provision of
clothing, shelter, and food.

Enable us, we pray, to be near to our fellow human
beings, even as you are near to us....Amen.

Daniel J. Theron

Unanswered Prayer

O God, you hear and answer prayers, but sometimes there seems to be no answer and no communication. At such times enable us to stop asking questions, and instead to listen and to reason. Enable us to surrender our own stubborn desires, hopes, and aspirations that may be the very noise that drowns out what you have to say. Grant us the willingness, we pray, to remove the rubbish of this world that clutters our hearts, our minds, and our lives, and that blocks out even your voice within us. And if there is still no clarity, grant us such faith in your fatherly love, your omniscience, and your providence that we may have the patience to wait until we ourselves would know better....Amen.

AUGUST

Tolerance

Lord, you created our world with such a multitude of people that we do not know, let alone understand. Even where we live we are surrounded by so many people who are different from us. Often we are influenced by rumors and judgments of others that we hear. Fill us with a spirit of tolerance towards others, we pray. Grant that it will deliver us from hasty and false conclusion and unwarranted condemnation. Liberate us from self-righteousness and bigotry. Instead let your love for others rule in our hearts, we pray, because they are all your children, even as we are....Amen.

Ordering our Lives

Almighty God, you are the beginning of all things, old and new. We come to you knowing that no secrets are hidden from you. You know us as we rise and as we sit down. We confess that we often neglect to use our abilities and our talents with which you have graciously endowed us; that we refuse to deal with our fears that hinder us; that we deny our shortcomings that often disable us. Enable us to excel where we have been endowed with talents and abilities, to put fear and doubt aside, to recognize our shortfalls, and to overcome all of these as we use the many gifts which you have graciously bestowed upon to us.

Reveal to us the solutions for the problems that might beset us. Show us direction for the inspiration that throbs within us.

And so, O Lord, enable us to take hold of the future anew without fear, without wavering, and without hesitation, but driven by hope, vision, faith, and great enthusiasm, we pray....Amen.

Illness

O God, our Creator and our sustainer, we thank you that you have made us with such wonderful bodies in which we spend our lives on this earth. We complain when we have to put up with a cold, or some other bouts that would pass shortly with ease, and we forget millions of others whose bodily home malfunctions with still incurable diseases, cancer, multiple sclerosis, and many other afflictions that bring real suffering.

We thank your for the marvels of medical research penetrating to the very essence of our existence, for all who seek our physical well-being-the researcher, the physician, the dentist, the nurse, and many others, tucked away and unseen, who minister to us when we are ill. We thank you for hospitals and other institutions that provide a haven of care for us, be we physically, or mentally ill.

When we need special care, grant wisdom to those who minister to us. Strengthen our trust in them, but especially in you. Grant us patience, optimism, and a good sense of humor so needed for our recovery.

And when recovery is not in the future, grant us the assurance that, whether in life or in death, there is always light, and there may even be a rainbow on the other side of every dark cloud.

And thanks be to you, our Great Physician....Amen.

Death

Our Father, we know that sometimes there is no recovery from illness, or old age, or accident in store for us. And when we realize that life will not be prolonged, grant us the contentment to acquiesce in the knowledge that by your grace we came into this world, and at your summons we depart from it to our eternal dwelling place. Grant us thankful hearts that we have been chosen and privileged, even for a short time, to live in a beautiful world which you have provided for us as our home, surrounded by the marvels and splendor of the universe, the work of your hands. Strengthen our faith, sharpen our spiritual vision, and light the torch of hope within us to see the unseen that is beyond our earthly sojourn and pilgrimage. May we then in faith and in great expectation hear the distant triumph song of hope breaking upon our ear at the end of life's rainbow, and rejoice in your covenant with us as we from the shores of etenity set sail for the beyond.

So, may your peace that passes all understanding become an eternal reality in our hearts. And to you be glory and thanksgiving for the gift of life forever....Amen.

Daniel J. Theron

Human Limitations

Almighty God, thank you for the ability to perform the many tasks necessary for the sustenance of life and for progress in the world around us. Yet, we are aware of our limitations and failures in so many ways. Therefore, protect us, we pray, where we can not protect ourselves; provide for us where we can not provide for ourselves; plan for us where we can not plan for ourselves; guide us where we can not see; when heart falters and we are despondent, be our courage and inspiration; when mind falls short, grant insight and wisdom; when weakness overtakes us, be our strength and staff. Surrounded by the comforting fellowship of your presence, grant us the will inasmuch as within us lies, to work out our own salvation, spurred on to do so with fear and trembling, knowing that you are working in us. Crown what we are able to purpose in your name with the blessing of success and rejoicing, we pray....Amen.

Providence in our Lives

Great is your faithfulness, O Lord, unto us. You ordained the universe of which we are a part, and it obeys your laws. You created the world with safeguards in its atmosphere to shield us from harm that would otherwise penetrate our earthly abode. You have blessed the earth with sunshine, wind, lightning, rain, and snow that it may bring forth to overflowing. You have planned the joy of spring that new life and beauty may burst forth after a long rest. You ordered the heat of summer that plants may wax to full fruition. You fashioned the splendor of autumn when we may reap the harvest of summer. Even the cold of winter is a gift from you that earth and plant may rest and be refreshed. You have ordained the sun to rise at its appointed time that with it we may order our lives for labor. And you have determined when night should come that we may rest for refreshing of body and mind, ready to welcome yet another new day when a fresh morning will burst upon us! As we contemplate it all, great indeed is your faithfulness, O Lord, unto us!...Amen.

Confession

Almighty God, our Father, whose love is extended to us at all times, we confess our fears, because of our unbelief, and our jealousies, because others have more than we do, our craving for bread that does not satisfy, and our greed that makes for strife on the face of the earth.

We would truly be contrite and purified that, created in your image, you may dwell in the hearts of your children, that we may be blessed with the gift of bringing tranquility where we have caused uproar, happiness where we have brought about suffering, peace where we are making war, prosperity where we have caused adversity, and the gift of joy where we may have been the reason for sadness and sorrow....Amen.

Harmony in the World

Almighty God, we thank you that you are the Father of the family of mankind and the ruler of all nations.

We are grateful for the wholesome influence of religion and worship through the ages as you have revealed it to many in diverse ways. We thank you for its call to strengthen the fabric of society with high ideals of goodness, civility, a common concern for fellow human beings, love, and hope eternal.

Give us the strength, we ask, to triumph over the forces of evil within ourselves that threaten the harmony and unity of the human race and of people with diverse origins-endless greed for material things, unbridled lust for power, the ravages of war, the shame of injustice, the horror of terrorism, the blemishes of crime.

Grant us peace and tranquility for progress, and above all renew your love in the hearts of your people to strengthen unity all over the face of the earth, we pray....Amen.

Opportunities

Almighty God, our Father, we thank you for opportunity that has knocked and is still knocking at our doors from day to day. Grant us keenness of ear to hear those knocks, willingness to open the door, and above all readiness to go out and to do what opportunity calls us to do.

And when there are no knocks at the door, endow us with courage and inspiration to go out and knock on doors ourselves, above all to open closed doors, and to find opportunities that have been hidden behind doors that have been mossed over of many years....Amen.

SEPTEMBER

Our Work in the World

C.A. DeMorest

Almighty God, whose power is never at rest in your creation, we believe in and we are ready to do your work in the world as your co-workers. To the end that this our commitment may become a reality, make us the water that flows, rather than the sand that shifts;

make us strong and enduring like the oak that towers in the forest, rather than mushrooms, fleeting, languishing, and dying in the shade. And so make us part of the power of your Kingdom in the world, we pray....Amen.

Courage

Our Father, sometimes we are beset by adversity and disappointment. The future seems to fade away, and the burden of life becomes too heavy. Mercifully wipe out our insecurity by a firm assurance that, even as the past rests in your hand, so also does your hand rest on the tiller of the future, and that you have the whole world in your hands. Grant that our awareness of your enduring love for us shall be renewed from day to day, and that we shall eagerly grasp the staff of faith and the torch of hope to gain courage, vision, and power. At whichever stage of life we find ourselves, give us the patience, we pray, to wait for the mist to clear and for new vistas to dawn beyond and beyond....Amen.

Beginning of the Academic Year

O God, source of all knowledge and wisdom, we commend to you at this time of the year the millions of children and young people returning to schools, colleges, universities, and other institutions of learning.

We thank you for the great privilege of education of which millions the world over are still deprived.

We thank you especially for those whose lives are dedicated to academic pursuits and instruction, for those who see to it that a sound mind lives in a sound body, for all staff burdened with administration and guidance, and for those, not the least of all, who help keep the roof from leaking, floors under feet shining, the lawns mowed, and food on the plates in the cafeterias or dining rooms.

Grant that factual knowledge, gained in the learning process, will yield satisfaction, aid in the growth of wisdom, and in the end build good and productive citizenship.

And as those who learn gain knowledge, may they discover the greatest truth of all-that the fear of the Lord is the beginning of wisdom....Amen.

Labor Day

Almighty God, your hand is at work around us at all times. We commend to you the millions all over the face of the earth who go forth to their labors from day to day: The plowman who tills, sows, and gathers in; the shepherd who feeds his flock; the herdsman who tends his cattle; the fishermen who harvest the seas; the miners who wrest riches deep from the bosom of the earth; the factory worker who bends over the assembly line; the computerists who keep track of a million things, the executive who manages from behind a desk; the salesmen who is on the road; the teacher who leads in front of a class.

We acknowledge our indebtedness to many hands unseen, even in distant places that provide the luxury, the comforts, and the sustenance that we enjoy every day, and which we so often take for granted.

As we gratefully acknowledge our dependence on all who labor in the world around us, many unnamed, we would above all acknowledge with gratitude our dependence on you, Lord and master worker over us all.

Grant, we pray, that our labors for earthly needs will be exceeded by our labors for things unseen and eternal, your Kingdom on earth....Amen.

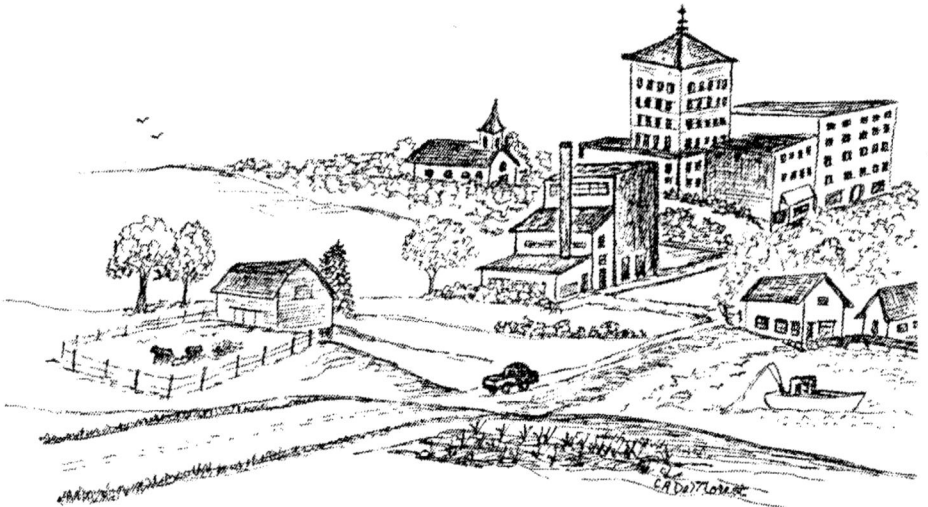

Admiration of Others

Almighty God, our Father, we thank you that you have endowed each of us with talents and abilities to employ in our diverse callings that have been assigned to us. To some you have given five talents, to others two, and to some only one. Whatever we have received, grant us the wisdom to invest and apply wisely and to enhance what we have. And when others would be more talented than we are and excel us, may we be great enough to admire them with praise rather than to stoop under a burden of jealousy and envy. Grant that it will be sufficient for us in the end to await your commendation, "Well done, well done, good and faithful servant."...Amen.

Adversity in Life

Almighty God, our Father, the wind is not always behind our backs and the sun does not always shine gently upon us. When it is dark and gloomy, the road steep, and the rain beats in our faces, cause a ray of hope to shine in us, strengthen our muscle of faith, increase our reservoir of knowledge and trust that you are always near us in all our adversities, and that the light of your face is ever over us to dispel gloom and distress, and to shine over us. So increase our inner strength to tackle, and one by one, to turn our adversities into victories. Hear this our prayer, O Lord, we ask....Amen.

C.A.DeMorest

Laborers In the Vineyard

Almighty God, we thank you that you have established communions the world over striving to advance the coming of your Kingdom. We thank you that these communions provide a spiritual home for each one of us. As we tread the ways of our daily lives, striving to do your Kingdom's work in the world, strengthen us so to equip ourselves that we may be better able to serve others. Make our fellowship so strong that together we all may be able to turn sadness into rejoicing; to see opportunity in disappointment, and even in disaster; to conquer evil with good; in faith to traverse the rivers on our way; to scale the mountains in life bravely and with courage; to attain to the clear summits beyond mist, travail, and labor; to behold the mystery of your great and glorious purposes, so often hidden from us, but of which you have nevertheless graciously selected us to be a part.

Grant that in confidence of faith we may know and pursue your designs and your goals for mankind. Let our work be dedicated not only to the growth and perfection of these communions as part of your Kingdom on earth, but above all as part of your Kingdom to come.

To accomplish the tasks of our fellowships to which we have been summoned in the world, bestow upon us the silent power of leaven and the invincible faith of a mustard seed, we pray....Amen.

Seekers and Sailors

Almighty God, our Father, we thank you that you have so created us as to be seekers and finders. We are grateful for the multitude of discoveries of past centuries that make our lives so comfortable and so easy.

As we seek, safeguard us, we pray, from the temptation to find and to cast anchor for ever in the harbors of self-satisfaction and contentment that will expose us to moth, rust, decay, regression, and disintegration. Instead inspire us, to set sail always for distant horizons that lie beyond and beyond in keeping with the destiny set for our lives on earth....Amen.

No Finality

Almighty God, our Father, in whom there is no finality, since we have been created by your Spirit, grant that we shall never accept finality in our own lives. Whether we are playing an ordinary game, or whether we are engaged in an important undertaking, teach us, we pray, that losing and failure nurture stamina and insight, and that victory and success are intended to generate inspiration to strive and to attain to higher goals. Although sometimes difficult to perceive, grant us patience and wisdom to wait until we learn that what looks like an end and finality in itself is only a fresh beginning, and applies even to the end of our earthly existence. ....Amen.

Moving on with History

Almighty God, we thank you that you have been and still are at the helm of the history of the world and its people as they move on through the circling years, and that your revelation to mankind is never at rest. Therefore, grant, we pray, that our faith shall neither retrench to the past, nor stand still in the present, but that it shall ever move on boldly into the future even as the truth continues to be made known to us in diverse ways. Grant us such wisdom that we shall not make the horizons of bygone years and ages our goals, but that we shall have the courage to turn around, bravely to sever the ties of the past where we must, and joyfully with hope to fix our sights on the beckoning vistas of tomorrow, eager to be a part of your presence and revelation in history, lest we become obstructions in the coming of your Kingdom....Amen.

The Olympiad

Almighty God, ruler of all nations, we thank you for the celebration of the Olympiad that comes around every four years, bringing together athletes of many nations from all over the world for sport, competition, and fellowship; for the exuberance of thousands who compete; for their examples of fitness, dedication and perseverance to render their best; for the demonstration of unity as many flags wave and compete. We are grateful to you that nevertheless, they march together as one with loyalty to the banner of the Olympiad.

Grant that their example of unity will inspire the nations of the world also to rally under a banner with loftier and worthier ideals-the banner of goodwill, harmony, and peace for all, we pray....Amen

OCTOBER

Autumn

Almighty God, whose art is so clearly painted on the canvas of nature around us, we come to you to give thanks for the fullness and glory of summer that we always so richly enjoy; for the abundance of summer's harvest, supplying in much of our needs; for the beauty of autumn, a magnificent work of art to warm our hearts.

In your providence plant and tree are finishing their appointed cycles. So also, as pilgrims on our own appointed courses and spans of human life, may we bear fruit in the wisdom of experience, in the beauty of a calm spirit and a clear mind-whatever our conditions of life-be it joy, or adversity.

And now as the summer has culminated in the splendor of autumn leaves, mingling the magnificent facets of amber, gold, scarlet, brown, and green so above all, may we, as we journey through life, mature as beautiful people in the satisfaction of accomplishment, in the gold of wisdom, in the purity of righteousness, and above all in the beauty of holiness.

For the multitude of lessons and examples of nature so readily available around us, and of which are a part, we come and we give thanks....Amen.

Heritage and Pride

Almighty God, our Creator, we thank you for the security of the heritage into which each one of us has been born. As we are filled with pride of our nationality, our race, our religion, our creeds, our family, open our eyes to the wideness of your mercy the world over, including all your children regardless of nationality, race, religion, or creed. So liberate us, we pray from bigotry, and enable us to lose our petty and selfish interests, for these are not part of your Kingdom....Amen.

Leaders by Example

O God, our Father, we thank you for the footsteps and voices of those among us who silently and without ostentation lead by their examples rather than by lofty positions; for those whose devotion to duty is the same whether they are assigned small duties, or whether they are summoned to great and demanding tasks; for those who use their allotted talents to their full extent for the benefit of those around them, be their toil sometimes ever so humble. We thank you especially for those who patiently and courageously set examples among us even in the shadow of a daily cross. Grant us, we pray, keenness to recognize those among us who excel in setting examples, and to gain from them inspiration to spur us on to nobler service in your Kingdom....Amen.

God's Presence With Us

Almighty Father, although you are far beyond our comprehension and even our imagination, we thank you that nevertheless you are our provider, our protector, and even our constant companion as we journey through life.

When we are infants, you provide loving arms to sustain us.

You protect us when daring the perils of youth.

You help shoulder the burdens of adulthood when we are faced with the responsibilities of parenthood, the pressure of daily toil, and the struggle against evil, within ourselves, or in the world around us.

You rejoice with us, when we are glad; you laugh with us, when we are happy; you understand and comfort when we mourn.

When the shadows of life are lengthening, you provide a rod and a staff to support us.

And in the end our eternal home is with you.

Thanks be to you for the unspeakable gift of your presence and nearness to us always....Amen.

God In History

Eternal God, Lord of history, we thank you for our ancient heritage handed down to us through many millennia; for the written word that preserved our traditions; for the host of witnesses, leaders, priests, judges, kings, and prophets, but especially for your revelation that came through Jesus Christ; for apostles and evangelists who heeded his call; for the host who have since followed in their footsteps through the ages, heroes of the Christian faith, some subjected to bonds, persecution, even death that we may enjoy the freedom into which we have been liberated; for your Church in which their witness has found stature and meaning, and for other communions and their wholesome influence on humanity.

As we witness to our faith in our own time, may your presence create in us the same devotion and commitment, which also inspired the forebears of our faith, that we may rightly interpret and hand down to future generations both old and new traditions, and so to build the future.

Grant, we beseech you, as we seek to preserve and pass on traditions of merit, that we shall not be so mired in the past as not to recognize new revelations made known to us through research of Scriptures and even secular science, for you are in all phases of history, putting new wine into new wineskins.

May our awareness of your presence in history throughout all the ages, even our own age, equip us better in love to labor for the coming and establishing of your Kingdom on earth. And to your great name be all honor, glory, and thanksgiving-always....Amen.

Gratitude and Confession

O God, our Father! We acknowledge that we have so much for which to be thankful; that there is so much of which we can be proud.

We can not but regret that we also have so much about which we need to be not only disturbed, but greatly upset.

103

We confess that we have even more to be ashamed of in the world around us, and perhaps within ourselves than we would even want to think about, let alone admit.

Grant that our gratitude and our sense of righteousness will more than enable us to confess and correct what disturbs us and remove what is unacceptable in your sight, we pray....Amen.

Mourning

O God, in your hands are the limits of our lives. From you we come and to your mansions we return at the end of our days.

We are saddened by death, and even more so by sudden, or tragic, or unexpected departure from our midst. Nevertheless, we thank you that you have granted to all of us and to those who leave us the unspeakable privilege of life in our beautiful, earthly home, to see and enjoy the marvels of your handiwork-stately, green trees, the majesty of mountains, the fragrance of flowers at our feet, the happy song of the bird on the wing, the splendor of sunrises and sunsets, and the grandeur of the star-lit firmament and endless space around us.

And now when the end has come in great sadness and we stand in dismay, aid us, and especially loved ones left behind, to understand, at least vaguely, and even to accept that the very storms in life are often but the dust of your feet. Grant us the faith and the hope to know that dust will settle and that the warmth of your presence will dispel the clouds.

Hear Our Prayers And Hymns, O Lord, We Pray

As you provide in the earthly needs of even the lowest of your creatures, fulfill in us the hope of eternal life that throbs in every heart.

Hear us as in silence we stand before you with our own thoughts and our tributes....Amen.

The Ministry

Eternal God, our Father, we thank you for those in ages past-a multitude unnumbered-whom you have summoned in the world to make teaching and proclaiming your word their vocation of life. We thank you for their courage to have gladly faced many dangers and hardships untold, some even paying with their lives for their convictions; for standing at lecterns, in pulpits, under trees, or even in open fields, whenever called upon during days and times of worship to declare the message of redemption all over the face of the earth. We commend to you all those in our own time on whose shoulders the burden of their mantles has fallen, who have heard your call, supreme and clear, to continue that great tradition boldly in a world so often wont to live apart from you and unredeemed. Through these your servants may your Kingdom continue to come, and your blessings to your people always abound, we pray....Amen.

Dedication

O Lord, we thank you that your laws for the conduct of our lives have been revealed to us in many ways. We have no excuse but to commit ourselves and to be dedicated. Having been so committed and dedicated, create in our hearts through your powerful presence in and around us, the urge and desire to place principle above personal gain; honesty above material advantage. And when we have so chosen, meet our resolve with your unfailing support through your inspiration. When we stumble, or fall, hand us the staff of faith, that we may rise up and labor on as those answering a supreme calling and a supreme mission in life, whatever our callings may be. And when distress of life is about to overwhelm us, revive in us the inspiration of hope that can discern vistas of the future, beckoning us to labor on. Grant that in the end, in your name, we may triumphantly rejoice in victory. So we pray.

....Amen.

Communion of Believers

Let us give thanks for the many wonders of the world in which we are citizens.

But on this day, let us especially give thanks for the wonder of Christianity, and for many other wholesome communions of believers which have survived and grown from age to age in spite of dungeon, fire and sword.

Let us give thanks for disciples, humble folk, who went out driven by God's presence in them to tell the good news of the love of God, of salvation, and of life eternal.

Let us give thanks for the learned Pharisee, Paul, whose life was totally transformed on the Damascus road to become a giant missionary who knew no rest but to proclaim the mystery of divine revelation, of the communion of believers, and of God's Kingdom, who founded the fellowships of many communions in spite of peril, persecution, and suffering.

Let us give thanks for many through the ages who have heard God's call to establish and strengthen the fellowship of believers in the world;

For the simplicity of its message;

For the comfort of its fellowship;

For the mystery of its sacraments;

For the communion of saints, visible and invisible;

For millions of the invisible communion for whom the strife of this life is over, whose earthly rest is around sanctuaries, in cemeteries, and others whose resting places are known but to God alone.

Let us give thanks for edifices of worship- majestic, or humble- witnesses in the world to the glory of God;

For their steeples that point us to a world beyond;

For their sanctuaries where the faithful and sinner alike commune with God in silence and peace;

Let us give thanks for communions the whole, wide world over which have heard God's voice in a mode different from ours;

Let us give thanks for the wideness of God's mercy that includes in his Kingdom, present and to come, all who hear and heed his voice and calling.

Let us pray that God would save from folly those to whom he has entrusted his revelation, his truth, and his people.

Let us pray that God shall grant victory to his Church and to other like communions everywhere in their struggles on earth to make the presence of his Kingdom more real; that in the end they may lose themselves in God's reign, and that communions of his children, with their tasks fulfilled, shall at last also come to rest in his Kingdom.

And to the Almighty be all honor, and praise, and glory for ever and ever....Amen.

Christianity

Let us give thanks to God Almighty for Christianity that rose like a Phoenix from the ashes of a crucifixion, desolation, and death to fly all over the world with a new message of salvation;

Let us give thanks that despondency of those left behind was transformed by the inspiration of God's Holy Spirit into boldness and courage to bring the new message of the Christian faith to a world that was so sorely in need of light in its darkness;

Let us give thanks for the vision of Jesus Christ and those who had followed him that a fulness of time had come, that the old had run its course, and that new wine had to be poured in new wineskins; for the Apostle Paul to whom God gave a new vision and interpretation of the life of Jesus Christ; for his indefatigable zeal and energy that marked his calling to bring the Gospel to distant places, despite persecution and much suffering;

Let us pray for the Church which is the guardian and trustee of Christianity: that it will never shy away from the truth, even if it means rejecting what it had earlier thought to be the truth, but proven otherwise; that God will safeguard it from being in a rut, incapable of grasping visions of new revelation, and unable to adapt to needed changes, able to give new direction in times of confusion; that God will

grant it unity of purpose under the protection of the
wideness of his mercy in spite of many divisions;

Let us pray that divine guidance, wisdom, and
vision will always prevail;

Let us pray for all in the world who climb the high
and steep mountain in search of what may come from the
other side of the mysterious veil that separates us
from the divine, be they theologians, or scientists in
seeking to understand the mysteries that underlie
God's revelation in Scriptures and in creation.

And when there are startling discoveries, let us
pray not to alienate reason and lose so many who go
through life uneasy and even estranged without the
comfort and support of Christian fellowship, who could
otherwise contribute so much to its labors;

Let us pray for the liberation of those who are
chained to the past, and who want to make the past the
future, comfortable in their armchairs of self-
satisfaction, but really on the slopes of regression.

Let us pray that the urgency of a fulness of time
will be recognized when it is upon us, and to respond
to its challenges with the same inspiration of divine
Holy Spirit, even as in the days of Jesus Christ and
his Apostles, and once again, to pour new wine into
new wineskins;

Let us pray, when a fulness of time has come, for
the wisdom and courage to file away in cherished
albums of history what is outdated and a hindrance to
the march of Christianity into the future.

Let us pray that the Phoenix of Christianity will
never be kept captive by any organization, even the
Church, but always be free to continue its journey
over the whole world for the Kingdom of God.

Let us pray that Christianity will always be free of shackles to lead at the new frontiers of the world, to challenge the world, rather than to wait in the rear for the world to challenge it.

And to the Almighty, by whose mercy and grace Christianity and its fellowship of believers came into being and have survived the centuries, be all honor, and glory, praise, and thanksgiving, always.

....Amen.

Government/Elections/Leadership

Almighty God, we come to you with troubled hearts and disturbing concerns in our national life, in particular in our government, the size of which staggers even wild imagination. Debt has increased for many a year to staggering proportions. This good land that you have entrusted to us, and what we earn have been mortgaged with burdens for generations to come. We are plagued by the outrage of self-serving politics with disregard for the common good, with promises to win elections that will burden us even more, open doors for corruption that lead to disrespect for the truth. We witness frequent lack of accountability in leadership. The abuse of power is a threat to us. The precious gift of freedom that you have so graciously bestowed upon us, is often misused to enslave us.

Nevertheless, we thank you for many in government who are people of character, honest people, for so much that is desirable and wholesome around us, for those who are the salt of the earth. We beseech you that their influence will permeate, not only our society, but also our government.

Hear Our Prayers And Hymns, O Lord, We Pray

As we are about to elect another government, grant that we shall have candidates whose sense of responsibility will far out pace their enjoyment of liberty and the luring temptation of self-seeking through means that are less than honorable, lest in the end our precious possession of freedom becomes null and void.

Grant that we shall with grave responsibility, preparation, and sound judgment exercise our privilege of electing those to whom we will entrust the honor to rule for us....Amen.

Daniel J. Theron

NOVEMBER

Elections

Almighty God, ruler of all nations, you have granted us freedom, the privilege and right to choose those who will rule over us as a nation.

We commend to you those who have made themselves available for office. And now that we have exercised our right, we remember those who have gone down in disappointing defeat. We thank you for their courage, for they have already served in bringing to us divergent points of view and different solutions to the problems that we face as a nation and a world.

Grant that we shall demand integrity and high moral character of all whom we elect to govern.

Grant us civility in government that rancor shall have no place, that dominance of a majority shall be moderate, and opposition of a minority shall be tempered for progress in government, for the benefit of our land, and for the good of us all.

We specially commend to your care those on whose shoulders now rests the great burden of responsible, representative government. Grant that their elevation to office shall be to them a summons to humility of service. Inspire them, we pray, with a sense of justice, fairness, and honesty as they seek to lead, to guide, and to direct, even to do your bidding, the Great Ruler of all, that we may indeed be a nation of prosperity, compassion, love, liberty, and justice for all....Amen.

God, our most merciful Father, we acknowledge the inability of our minds to reach beyond the veil of our mundane existence; the callousness of our hearts where we should repent or have compassion; our human desires to be self-serving without you; our lack of devotion to further your Kingdom and to establish the laws of love and justice; our neglect to permeate our day with the Good News of salvation in word and in deed. So often there is no spiritual health in us, and so we create a devil within ourselves and in the world. O Lord, grant us your forgiveness; grant us your salvation, and above all, the inspiration of your presence in us always to lead lives more acceptable to you, we pray....Amen.

Veterans' Day

Lord, our God, we come on this Veterans Day to lament that war has ravaged the world through many centuries. Nevertheless, we must also come to thank you for the courage and willingness of many who have served to protect the boundaries, and freedom of their own countries, and the freedom and rights of their fellow human beings in many places in this world.

We mourn many whose light of life was snuffed out in battle while it was still day. We give thanks for many who have survived while in harm's way. We would hold in high honor those who returned home maimed and crippled for life. And so we commend to your mercy all those who have survived with loss of limb, and who continue to suffer discomfort and pain. We thank you for those who ministered to them while in battle and who continue to tend to their needs.

As many on this day recall with sorrow and sadness the loss of comrades and loved ones in the horror of war, grant them the comfort of your love, and your consolation that time will heal the wounds of memory.

Above all we thank you that for all veterans the roar of guns, cannons, aircraft, and missiles has at last echoed away over now silent battle fields.

Grant, O Lord, that their courage, bravery, and sacrifices shall not have been in vain, but that brotherhood, love, and peace may eventually reign on the face of the earth for the honor, glory, and praise of your great name....Amen.

The Kingdom of God

Let us give thanks for the mysteries of the Kingdom of God that are hidden in all of his creation; for God's power that governs the universe around us and guides the firmament in its course, even the sun, the moon, and the stars; for its presence not only in governing the masses of billions of celestial bodies, but also steering our small and insignificant planet as part of the universe; for the marvels of the world around us-the wind, the rain, the trees, the drop of water, the infinitesimal components of matter on which we set our feet; for the gift of life on this beautiful earth.

Let us give thanks that God's Kingdom has been made known to mankind in the past and that it is still being revealed to us from day to day in new revelations: in the whisper of electricity, in the thunder of nuclear power, in all the wonders of science and research that have been revealed to us.

Let us give thanks that God's Kingdom is not beyond our reach, but that it has also been revealed to us in the words of prophet and apostle, and many sages in many lands through many centuries; that it has always been in human history and is present in our midst continuously.

Let us give thanks that the law of God's Kingdom to govern our lives was revealed to us in the ten commandments of love and in sacred word.

Let us, not only during the advent season, but at all times give thanks for the revelation of the Kingdom of God in the coming of a little child in the world and in the life and teachings of Jesus Christ.

Let us, above all give thanks that the reign of the Kingdom of God is forever and ever, and that it can have a place in our hearts even today, and always.
....Amen.

Thanksgiving/Harvest Home

1

Let us give thanks that God is the provider in all our needs.

At this time as we give thanks for the harvest that has been gathered in, let us come to give thanks for pilgrims and pioneers, who despite perils of the seas, came to this land with undaunted faith and faced the challenge of uncharted and threatening frontiers before them; for their perseverance, steadfastness, and trust; for their example of gratitude and thanksgiving.

Let us also give thanks for millions, who through the circling years have followed bravely in their footsteps to these shores.

And again for other millions who have braved the unknown wilderness of this land to settle it at the peril of their own lives, and to make it productive. Let us give thanks for indigenous inhabitants with whom we now form one nation under divine guidance.

Let us give thanks that, through the sacrifices of our forebears, through their toils, frugality, and faith in divine providence, we have been blessed as a nation with abundance and wealth far beyond their and even our own expectations, and far exceeding what we deserve.

Let us give thanks for the plenty of this land and all our comforts that have freed many productive minds for research, development, and creation.

Let us give thanks that in our time, because we are heirs of the fruit of their labors, we ourselves have arrived as pilgrims at the vast and frightening, new frontiers of the electronic age, the nuclear age, the space age, the age of wonder drugs, wonder surgery, and the age of genetic engineering.

In addition to giving thanks at this festive time for all the benefits accorded us through the centuries, let us above all pray that Almighty God may grant our generation a generous harvest of wisdom, patience, vigilance, moral stamina, and a sense of responsibility, lest we become arrogant and destroy ourselves. Let us pray that generations to come may also give thanks for our generation as undaunted and daring, as wise, with foresight, but above all, as putting our trust in Providence, even as the first settlers and pioneers had done.

Let us give thanks for God's goodness to his people through the centuries and for his unfailing sustenance in what has been provided liberally for millions this day, on millions of tables across the land, even on our own.

Let us in true humility for what we so richly enjoy give

THANKS TO ALMIGHTY GOD. Amen.

2

Let us give thanks for the splendor of scarlet, and the glory of gold in the hills;
For the crispness of autumn air piping its paeans through the trees;
For chrysanthemums swaying on supple stems;
Pumpkins watching at the door;
Indian corn clustered and knocking at the door;
Pine cones at the hearth waiting.
Let us give thanks for the harvest safely gathered in.
Let us give thanks to the Lord of the harvest, who has provided for us like the true Father.
Let us humble ourselves before him in this season of bounty
With the homage of our thanksgiving:
For labor crowned with joy;
For fields that once again yielded their abundant increase-
For the plenty of the land in which we live by God's providence;
For millions of folk unseen and forgotten, but by God,

Who go about their duties to provide in our daily needs, humble and true;

For those who gather in the abundance of the seas that guard our shores;

For those who from the bosom of the earth wrest its hidden riches,

And mold them for our use and pleasure;

For the mysterious powers implanted in God's handiwork around us,

Unleashed and harnessed to turn the wheels of industry,

And so to bless us with prosperity;

For those worthy of high office, of oversight, and of guidance;

For places of learning where the minds of our youth are made receptive to wisdom and a desire to seek and harvest the unknown;

For spires of sanctuaries-sentinels of mountain and plain-

Pointing our hopes and aspirations to the land of eternity.

Render us, O Lord, a nation worthy of all your benefits to us, we humbly pray....Amen.

3

God, our protector and our provider, we thank you that you set a table before us in all conditions of life, be it joy and gladness, be it adversity and sadness. But today we thank you that with millions across this land you have set before us a table of thanksgiving, thanksgiving for safe journeys, for the sun that shines, for the wind that blows, for the rain that falls, and for the snow that blankets the earth in the winter that it may rest, and in due time bring forth abundantly to provide in all our needs.

For the bounty of our own table, for our fellowship, for your fatherhood and providence that never fail we say: thanks be to you, and again, thanks be to you!...Amen.

Thanksgiving/Harvest Home/Advent

O Lord of the harvest, you have provided in our needs a harvest of substance like the true Father, and you are also providing in our spiritual needs a harvest of inner peace, comfort, redemption, and salvation.

We would offer the gratitude of our hearts:

For the fields that yielded their abundant increase-thirty-, sixty-, and one hundredfold;

For the plenty of the land in which, by your grace, we live.

We would give thanks for all those who harvest the hidden riches from deep beneath the earth, and for those who mold and apply them to the use of mankind;

For the fisherman whose harvest is in the deep of the oceans;

For the blaze of the furnace by which industry turns and creates a multitude of comforts of life for us;

For ten thousands of executives who know no rest, and likewise

For millions of little folk, who humbly go about their duties from day to day, whose labor produces the harvest of industry;

For all places of learning where the human mind reaps a harvest of knowledge and wisdom;

For all places of worship and for the spires of sanctuaries all over the face of this land and of the earth, pointing us beyond and to an even greater harvest and season of thanksgiving;

For the pealing of the message of Advent that will soon resound over vale and mountain;

For the coming of divine light in the world, especially through Jesus Christ, that the world may reap and enjoy the harvest of peace on earth, comfort, redemption, and salvation.

Above all do we come to you with thanksgiving for the greatest of all harvests-the coming of your Kingdom in the hearts of your people.

And to your great name, O Lord, for all that you supply in such abundance be all our true and humble Thanksgiving....Amen.

Daniel J. Theron

DECEMBER

A Day of Infamy

O God of peace, our Father, as we recall the anniversary of the Day of Infamy and as we lament barbarism that still stalks the human race, we acknowledge the darkness in which we and our world are often so deeply immersed.

We honor those whose lives were snuffed out without warning, many of whom found their final resting place is the depths of the ocean.

But we thank you for the contrast of the Advent season with its symbol of light to dispel darkness from the human heart. We give thanks especially for the birth of Jesus Christ, the hope of the world, the hope of redemption, peace, and goodwill on earth, that there shall be no more Days of Infamy....Amen.

A Prayer for Peace*

Almighty God, our Father, we earnestly pray for peace among the nations of the world. And as we do so, we confess that, because of our human frailty and shortcomings, the way to the mountain tops of peace and tranquility too often leads through valleys of pain and suffering, and even the horrors of war with bloodshed and tears. In your great goodness liberate us from intolerance, and alike of greed and want that make for strife and that cause nation to rise up against nation.

Hasten the day, we pray, when the evil of aggrandizement can be checked without warfare, and mercifully grant that contentment and love shall reign in the hearts of your people-everywhere-that we may be at peace with one another. Grant us such love and such wisdom that will bring about harmony among the nations in keeping with the splendor of this beautiful planet which you have graciously entrusted to us on our pilgrimage through life to the beyond....Amen.

*Written in January,1991 when the Iraqi War was threatening.

Revelation

Eternal Father, God of light, we thank you that although we do not know it all, we need not grope in total darkness, for you have revealed yourself sufficiently to mankind in many ways. Especially do we thank you for your revelation of love, faith, and hope as it came to the world through Jesus Christ so mysteriously to dwell in us to be a light unto our feet, and an inspiration for our hearts. Since you have manifested your unbound love to the world, let love so abound in our own hearts that we may love our neighbors even more than ourselves. Since you are the ultimate truth, keep us from shying away from it, ignoring it, or even contradicting it. Liberate us from narrow-mindedness by granting us a vision of the wideness of your mercy, and once we have seen it, strengthen in us how we believe, loving you with all our being. Confirm in us the hope of things unseen and eternal, we pray....Amen.

Hear Our Prayers And Hymns, O Lord, We Pray

Advent and Christmas[*]

1

Almighty and eternal Father, we thank you for revealing yourself to us in the form of a little child-in tenderness, in trust, and innocence; for teaching us that to such belongs your Kingdom.

We rejoice in all that makes this season so beautiful and so holy: its songs, its sacred music, and its lights that adorn our cities, our streets, our homes, and our sanctuaries. As these lights dispel the gloom of night around us, grant, we pray, that the light of the Christmas season may also drive away the darkness that may lurk in our own hearts. And so enable us together with the Christ child to be the light of the world, we pray....Amen.

2

Almighty God, Father of Jesus Christ and also our Father, we pause in the rush of a busy world, filled with our daily concerns, to give thanks for so many hallowed traditions of Advent and Christmas, all of which set this season apart and make it so unique for us and the world: for Christmas trees with treasured ornaments; for melodies and words of songs, secular

---

[*] The picture of the nativity according to the Gospel of James is one of the frescoes in Panagia Tou Arakou, a late twelfth century church in Cyprus. According to it Jesus was born in a cave. Joseph sits outside the cave with his donkey tied to a tree. At the bottom right Mary, we may assume, gives Jesus a bath. The writing is in Greek. The title in the middle reads "The birth of Jesus Christ." At the top right is Luke 2 : 10.
Reproduced with permission of the Byzantine Photograph Fieldwork Archives, Dumbarton Oaks, Washington, D. C.

and sacred, that take on new meaning each year to enliven the spirit of the season, to comfort us, and to inspire us that we may strive for what is lofty and eternal; for goodwill, for the custom of beautiful Christmas cards with greetings; for renewal of friendships with greetings, letters, and news; for gifts generously given by family and friends alike. Above all do we thank you for the innocence of a little child born in Bethlehem; for the divine found in the humble places of life, even a stable and a manger, and for light that came in the darkness of this world and in our own hearts....Amen.

3

Lord, grant that the celebration of the coming of the Prince of Peace may hasten the day when nations shall turn their armaments into plowshares and instruments of peace, instruments for preserving life, rather than destroying it, and make war no more.

As the world in solemn celebration recalls your revelation in Jesus Christ, expected by so few, grant that the redemption wrought by him shall cleanse the hearts of those touched by his life, and set an example for the world.

For greetings and remembrances of family and friends and for tables overflowing with abundance to mark our joy and our commemoration of this festive day, we bring to you honor, praise, glory, and thanksgiving today and always....Amen.

4

Almighty God, our Father, we thank you for a brief time of respite from the sometimes stark realities of life in the world around us, to indulge in the many things that make Christmas time so beautiful: Christmas trees and their dazzling array of decorations, the fantasies of Santa Claus, of reindeer in the skies, of Old King Wenceslas and his brave, little page. Thank you for a time when we can withdraw from the hurry of life to contemplate the unknown, the unseen, and even the miraculous in which you are willing to reveal yourself to us....Amen.

5

Lord, when this joyous time of Christmas is past, grant that we shall continue to carry the spirit of Christmas in our hearts, to heal in the world around us so many wounds caused by the tragedies of human existence-the tragedies of sorrow, of bloodshed, and of tears, that still afflict an endless number of our fellow human beings in spite of all the centuries of your message of love, salvation, redemption, liberty from bondage to evil, and peace.

Make us your instruments of the Christmas spirit throughout the year to come, we pray....Amen.

6

Almighty God, our Father, as the Jewish people celebrate Hanukkah and the Christians celebrate the birth of Jesus Christ, we thank you for the many hallowed traditions of this season that have been entrusted to all of us through the centuries. As we enjoy the festive lights of celebration that illumine our streets, our sanctuaries, and our homes, we especially thank you for the symbolism of light that expels the evil of darkness, that enlightens our hearts and our minds to know what is right; your eternal light that is a lamp unto our feet on life's pilgrimage.

Grant that your people shall be your light in the world, set on a hill that can not be hid, and that we shall press on for the coming and establishing of your everlasting Kingdom of peace and goodwill....Amen.

7

Almighty God, our Father, as we pause in a busy world, made busy by so many worldly concerns besetting us, we give thanks for the hallowed traditions that make this season so especially dear to us; for the innocence of a little child; for the divine that does not need palaces, but that comes to us in the lowly places of life, even a stable and a manger; for the gift of music that inspires this season with songs sacred and secular, sweeping us up into the spirit of celebration, comforting us, and lifting us up to reach for what is lofty and eternal; for goodwill, gifts, greetings, and love showered upon us by family and friends alike-near and far.

We rejoice in the lights that adorn our streets, our sanctuaries, and our homes. Grant that they will be symbols of the light that emanates from you to drive the darkness in the world away, and so to cleanse even our own hearts that we may be a light wherever we find ourselves.

Cause, we beseech you, that the celebration of the coming of the Prince of Peace may hasten the day when nations shall turn their armaments into instruments of peace, instruments of joy rather than instruments of destruction, and make war no more.

As the world in solemn adoration recalls your great revelation in Jesus Christ, grant that his redemptive work shall eventually reach people everywhere.

For rekindling of spiritual values in our own lives, and for the abundance that marks our joy and our celebration, we offer to you honor, praise, and glory, especially giving thanks for the coming of the Prince of Peace in the world....Amen.

Peace for Jerusalem

Let there be peace, Lord, for Jerusalem,
God of Christians, the Muslims, and the Jews.
"O little town of Behlehem, How still we see you lie."
"Peace on earth, good will to men,
From heaven's all gracious King."
And he shall be called, "Counsilor, Prince of Peace,"
Let there be peace where Jesus Christ was born.
"O star of beauty, star of night,"
Festive in our homes and bright,
Guide us through the night to peace....Amen.

Grace at a Meeting

1

Almighty God, Provider in all our needs, we thank you for the mystery of your Kingdom which is not confined to distant realms, but present with us already in everyday life, even as we break bread together. Bless this food to our bodies, our hearts and our minds that we may be a blessing to others, we pray....Amen.

2

Almighty God, our Father, we are grateful for the beauty of your handiwork all around us, a delight to the eye and the mind, for the earth that brings forth abundantly to provide in our physical needs, especially our daily bread. Accept, we pray, the gratitude of our hearts for your fatherhood and your providence that never fail....Amen.

Invocation at a Meeting

Our Father, we thank you that, in the midst of the splendor of your handiwork, our allotment has fallen in lovely places. Our pantries are full and our cups are filled to overflowing. As we enjoy the bounty with which your providence and fatherhood have favored us, make us the more eager to share it with others who are less fortunate than we are, we pray....Amen.

Inspiration

Our Father, when life comes at us with changes and decisions, sometimes very hard, equip us with wisdom, insight, and strength never to be wavering where we should be decisive. When disappointment, hardship, defeat, and pain come our way, let us not be despondent where we should be courageous. Enable us to forget our own adversities by lending a helping hand to others less fortunate than we are. When we are victorious and life is easy, make us humble, thankful,

Hear Our Prayers And Hymns, O Lord, We Pray
and an inspiration to others struggling on their
pilgrimage through life. At all times, we pray,
inspire us to lift our eyes to the horizon of hope,
steadfast as we strive for the high prize of the
upward call of salvation in your Kingdom....Amen.

Spiritual and Physical Needs

Our Father, we thank you that your Kingdom is not
confined to a realm far distant from us, but that it
is already present with us in everyday life; for the
Church and other like communions the world over that
labor to make your Kingdom more real in the darkness
that so often besets the world. We are grateful for
your presence in us, inspiring us to do your work in
the world; for the beauty of your handiwork around us
that makes our world a pleasant place for our earthly
sojourn; for the abundance of material things that
supply in our physical needs and make life
comfortable. So do we come to you with thanksgiving
for so much that we often take for granted: our
shelter, our garments, our daily bread, and even such
common needs as a piece of paper and a pencil to
write. Accept the gratitude of our hearts for your
everlasting arms which always encompass and undergird
us, we pray....Amen.

Launching into the Future

O Lord, allow us not in futility to wish back what
is past and gone by, but in faith and hope to launch
out into the future, although unknown to us. Inspire
our hearts with expectations, loftier than what

inspired us before, rooted in our trust that just as you have been our Father in the past, so you will be in time to come. As we proceed on the highway of life's journey, sometimes beset by disappointments and adversity while we labor and strive to accomplish our purposes, enable us never to despair. Strengthen us instead to take heart and to fashion all our endeavors to become part of your universal purpose and your plan for mankind. Support our weak hands with hope. Stay our wavering footsteps with faith in you and with an awareness that we are your coworkers in this world. So empower our hearts and minds that we may always advance steadfastly towards our goals inspired by zeal, high resolve, and hope, we pray....Amen.

PRAYERS BY GEORGE MURRAY PELLISSIER[*]

1

(Mt. 6:5-13)

"Heavenly Father, according to your word, 'Seek my countenance,' do we approach you as we bring to a close the activities of this day. We thank you for the privilege and the mind set to be able to do so. That you will draw near to us is a sure promise. Grant us uprightness and simplicity that we shall not be guilty of 'idle repetition of words,' of many words with many unknown meanings, which are often just the beginning of evading the truth. Mercifully safeguard and bring to fruition the good that emanated this day from thought, word, and deed, for you are the fountain and safekeeper of all the highest values of our lives. You are the ultimate guarantee and sanction of all of these, and done in your name, they can not be lost.

"Render us from day to day to be better co-workers with you by causing us more fully to understand, better to sense, and better to strive in the name of our Lord, Jesus Christ.

"Pardon us our debts as we will also pardon our debtors. For Christ's sake. Amen."

---

[*]George Murray Pellissier, one of those to whose memory this book is dedicated, was a highly respected, beloved, and revered Dean of the Theological Faculty, Section B, at the University of Pretoria, Republic of South Africa, where he taught various subjects, especially Systematic Theology. These prayers were most likely given, as the custom was, at the 11 p. m. conclusion of the day's radio broadcasts of the South African Broadcasting Corporation. He believed that prayer should be based on Scripture. The selection, given at the beginning of each prayer, was read with it. (Translated from Afrikaans by the present author)

133

2

(Dan. 9: 3 - 10)

"Almighty God, who keeps the covenant and shows mercy to those who fear your name, the nearer we come to you in the quiet of our heart, the more we become aware of our known and hidden wanderings-thanklessness for so much in life that accrues to us undeserved, the known disobedience which with open eyes went against your Spirit and your precepts, the known and unknown rebellion against serving you which is part of the best in us, the selfishness which would violate even the most holy for our own purposes. At the thought of all these things, so many and so varied, we must confess with the prophet: 'We have sinned and done wrong, we ourselves, those who rule over us, as well as our fathers.'

"But with the Lord, our God, there are mercy and forgiveness. He forgives abundantly those who draw near to him in faith dependent on the forgiveness earned by Christ. Lord, hear us! Lord, pardon us! Lord, please take note and do it. Do not tarry for the sake of your name which resounds over this land and over this nation. We ask it for Christ's sake. Amen."

3

(Ez. 37 : 3 - 11)

"Lord, our God, when the soul is at a low ebb and its voice is hoarse, saying: 'My expectation is lost; it is finished with me,' then your word comes to us: 'Look I will open your graves and raise you from your graves, O my people.' How often has your word once again been the foundation of our hope and expectation!

When what is good in us and our cleaving to it diminish and become doubtful due to sin and temptation of life, it is then that you again come to us with the word of hope and strength.

"You indeed are the ultimate hope and foundation, O hope of all the world. Grant that for those who have given up hope and for whom the world has begun to turn dark that there will be the dawn of a new hope, a new beginning, a new life with you and for you. In your love and in your faithfulness you will remember your covenant, you will open their graves. Do this in the name of him who himself by his death can open all graves, and who has always done it. Amen."

4

(Ps. 116 : 1-14)

"Lord, praised by your name! What can we render to you for all your benefits to us? Especially do we recall at this time that you have listened: that you have broken bonds, caused anxiety and concern to disappear. Our souls once again returned to their rest. For this especially do we give thanks.

"How dreadful, in retrospect would it have been, if you had not listened, and your hand had not helped. What tears and what stumbling would there not have been?

"Establish the resolutions which we have made in anxiety that they may become the fixed guidelines of life. Grant that the sun of new prosperity shall not shrivel these up. Enable us to keep our promises. Renew a steadfast spirit in our innermost being. O author of both the will and the completion of all that is good, grant that the feeling of gratitude will not fade away and lead to further weakening, but be the beginning of girding ourselves on anew. In the name of him who fought in prayer. Amen."

INVOCATIONS

1

Almighty God, our Father, whom the heavens of heavens can not contain, much less the temples and sanctuaries made by the hands of mortal, human beings, condescend, we pray, to fill this your house of worship with your presence. Make us aware of your nearness in our midst as Spirit in such fullness as our finite minds can comprehend and to which our limited emotions can respond that our hearts may anew reach out to you from whom we came.

Remove from our hearts and minds the concerns of this day that may beset us, and render our worship unfruitful. So liberate us from what is unworthy to be prepared indeed to worship you in Spirit and in truth, we pray....Amen.

2

Almighty God, our Father, we thank you that your presence is around us like a mantle. Yet at times we can not see or comprehend what it is all about. Eternal Spirit, make your presence more real to our searching hearts and finite minds as we seek to worship you this day; as we wait to hear what you want to say to us; as we seek to know your will; and as we sincerely desire to make your presence part of our daily lives. To that end, we pray, set us apart in this hour from all worldly influences. As we draw near to you in worship, liberate us from all worldly influences that continue to make undue claims on our

137

hearts and minds. So attune our entire being that we may indeed worship you in Spirit and in truth. ....Amen.

3

Almighty God, our Father, liberate us from the desire to seek you in the miraculous opening of the heavens, in the thunder clap, in the great rush of wind, or in the pillar of fire. May we come to know that you are in the ordinary things of life as well, in a friendly smile, in the giving of a cup of cold water, in the speaking of an uplifting word. Come this day, we pray, in your unmistakable, still, small voice of calm, that serene in spirit and in mind, we may fix our vision on the unseen, and gain a firmer hold on things eternal....Amen.

4

Almighty God, our Father, as this day summons us to worship you, open our eyes to what is beautiful that we may discern your hand in it; attune our minds to what is true and eternal that we may come to know you more fully; make our hearts sensitive to what is holy and divine, and so enable us to elevate our purposes and strivings in life far above the passing and the little concerns of our daily existence. Grant such an awareness of your presence as Spirit in us that in worshiping today, we may grow in the beauty of holiness....Amen.

5

Our God and our Father, you are the peace and comfort of the searching mind and soul. Remove from our minds the disquieting thought, the unworthy impulses of our hearts that seek to distract from the all-surpassing worth of your presence; wipe out the troubles of this day that seek to annul the inspiration of fellowship in your presence. And as we are touched by your nearness, make our hearts sensitive to things beyond our earthly life, that, in the midst of the clamor of the world around us, we may nevertheless hear even the low whisper of your voice of calm, know that you are God, and that we may indeed worship in such reverence and adoration as become your unspeakable majesty.

....Amen.

6

Lord, our God, we come to you on this day of rest and worship. Since the dawn of day, as the earth revolves around the sun, church bells have already pealed joyously all over the earth-be it from mighty cathedrals, from humble sanctuaries, or just a rusty plowshare hanging from a tree-to summon countless hosts of believers to gather in your presence, humble, joyful, and triumphant. And we would join with this host the whole world over to draw near to you and to seek your face. Create in us an awareness and tolerance of the great diversity of your people. Liberate us from prejudice and small-mindedness that your people, united and universal, may rise to their high and upward call in a world so deeply divided and so sorely in need of unity and redemption, including even ourselves....Amen.

7

Eternal God, to you must all flesh come; and we have come. Come to us in such clear accents that we can understand. As we seek to worship you, cleanse us from ignoble thoughts and remove all evil from our hearts, we pray. As we wait in great expectation for your word, be it in Scripture, in song, in prayer, in exposition, or even in silence, make us receptive in heart and mind that we may be strengthened in faith, obtain wisdom, find our rest in you, gain hope, and receive inspiration for the task of life that rests upon our shoulders....Amen.

8

Advent-Music Program

Almighty God, our Father, you are the source of all wisdom, all joy, and all beauty. At this season of advent we come to you, to bring our humble offering of thanksgiving, especially for those whom you have endowed with talents sensitive to the sublime; for their ability and inspiration to transform the yearnings of the heart into music and song-an uplifting joy to mankind, and an offering of praise and adoration to your great name. By the cleansing of your presence in us remove from your people all manner of evil that, sanctified, they may be made receptive to the spirit of the child of Bethlehem; that in lives of love, godliness, humility, and mercy the King of Kings may be born in us today....Amen.

140

9

Ordination / Installation

Lord, our God, through the centuries you have called special people in special ways away from the world to be holy and to be your own-the little lad Samuel, the monarch David, the Apostle Paul, and many others as prophets, apostles, evangelists, pastors, teachers, elders, deacons, Sunday School teachers, and laypeople in many different positions of service. Possess and purify every heart and every mind of us here assembled that what we do this hour in your name may be sanctified and established. So may we all be edified, and gain awareness of our own calling as laborers in the fields of your Kingdom. So revive in our hearts a new vision of our own calling and of your great and eternal purposes for the world in the Church and in your Kingdom.

Grant that this hour of consecration will become an hour of high resolve to follow in the footsteps of Jesus Christ-not to be ministered unto, but to minister....Amen.

10

Almighty and everlasting God, who is Spirit and who bears witness with our spirits that we belong to you, meet with us anew as we seek to draw near to you in worship. Bestow upon us that peace that passes all understanding. Allow not any unhallowed thought to defile the sanctity of our worship. Deliver us from all vain things. May we here gain wisdom, renew our staff of faith, rediscover your love in our hearts, strengthen our hope in things eternal and beyond, experience the influence of things unseen, find rest and comfort in you, and above all, renew our inspiration for life and the high calling to which you have summoned us....Amen.

PASTORAL PRAYERS

1

O God, our Father, how wonderful are your thoughts to us! How excellent is the sum of them! We would extol you as our God and our King. Everyday we would bless you and praise your name forever.

And therefore, O Lord, liberate us from all that would make us and our meditations unworthy. May self-exultation vanish in self-searching; may self-seeking and pride be turned into humility of confession, and into casting ourselves upon the mercy of your grace. Pardon us our unbelief that demands to know the whole way before taking the first step; our unwillingness to follow your guidance day by day. Let the balm of your forgiveness bring healing and peace to the penitent heart as we confess our shortcomings before you.

O Thou, whose fatherhood encompasses us, you have provided bountifully in all our needs; you have prepared for those who love you things that the eye has not seen, nor ear heard, nor entered into the thoughts of human beings.

We bring you the homage of our thanksgiving: for your Kingdom, heavenly and eternal, yet present with us in the small things of life; for lofty aspirations that it kindled in many before us; for the serenity of their holy lives; for the glimpse of eternity that inspired prophet and apostle alike, and through them still guides the footsteps of those who belong to you; for every noble expectation that enables us to nerve the wavering will, and to revive hope out of fear and despair that we may see the horizons beyond the mist in the valleys.

In your mercy bestowed upon us, may we all find unity in the service and in the up building of the Kingdom of heaven on earth. In this our common calling make us so confident in you that we shall not seek the esteem of human beings, but be content that you, our Father, know our hearts. Remove from us the desire for eminence that in the humility of foot washing we may prefer one another in honor, and in the surrender to selflessness we may live unsparingly to that which is divine.

And when the sound of our Christian calling grows dim in the tumult around us, may the inspiration of your presence infuse in us the will that will not fail, because our labor is not for ourselves, but for your Kingdom. And so make us truly sons and daughters of the prophets and of the apostles, worthy of the faith of our fathers, and above all worthy of the example of Jesus Christ, through whom we make these our prayers and our petitions....Amen.

2

How hallowed are the portals of your house, O Lord. In it even the sparrow finds a nest. As your people draw near to you, grant their hearts your heavenly rest.

Your holiness is roundabout you as a mantle of light, but we are unworthy and often in darkness. Hear us as we call upon you to liberate us and to forgive us. Pardon, we pray, the arrogance that dares to live without loving you with all our being and without due regard for those who are your children. We confess our suspicion of others, born out of the untrustworthiness of our own impure hearts; the prejudice against others in which we often seek to hide our own shortcomings. And if there be any undue seeking of authority, power, and eminence, pardon us. Teach us that you know our thoughts from afar off, be they worthy, or unworthy. In self-searching, bestow upon us that humility that will truly rend our hearts in penitence that we may be restored to the joy of your salvation.

Our Father, whose love and faithfulness patiently persevere with us, you have provided for us like the true Father. We thank you that in the revelation of Jesus Christ you have shown us the way to walk in this life and the road to life eternal. We thank you for his life and example: for always choosing the abiding values and putting lesser things in their true perspective; for despising hypocrisy and insincerity of motive, but exalting the pure heart and noble intention; for making your Kingdom a reality-even laying himself on the altar of redemption, that his loss may become our life. We thank you for those in whose lives his image is portrayed in our day-even in our midst.

Our Father, remember, we pray, the leaders of the nations. In great compassion upon your handiwork and your people, bestow upon them the wisdom that comes from you, the spirit of understanding, and such vision to conduct the affairs of the nations in accord with the encompassing and glorious purposes of your Kingdom, that the yearning for peace in the hearts of millions may grow into unity and brotherhood on the face of the earth.

145

As we go from this sanctuary, may we still all remain one in the bond of common allegiance that binds us together as followers of Jesus Christ and fellow laborers in the sowing and harvesting of your Kingdom- like our master, the great servant, gathering in those whom the world rejects and despises, because all your children are dear in your sight; proclaiming the presence of your reign in word and deed; building up the fellowship of believers; strengthening the weary, lest they faint; aiding those who are stumbling, lest they fall; seeking the lost, lest they perish; putting our confidence in you, lest we ourselves would fail.

And may we daily rest our hands in your hand and march with your Kingdom into the dawn of hope where expectation will be transformed into life eternal.

And to your great name be honor and thanksgiving always....Amen.

3

A Day of Prayer and Communion

Almighty God, whom the heavens of heavens cannot contain, much less the temples made by the hands of men, we would worship in your sanctuary and we would exalt you as our Father, for you did condescend to reveal yourself in Jesus Christ who walked among us as a humble servant, and you are still willing to dwell in the heart that would truly seek you.

And therefore, O most merciful Lord, who knows our coming in and our going out, would we acknowledge and confess before you that our transgressions, committed against you arrogantly, or unwittingly, are many. Deliver us from pride and arrogance; from tension and ill-feeling, if there be any; from all that may be an offense to the table of our Lord. We thank you that we can rest assured in your willingness to pardon and in the joy of your salvation that makes us whole.

Our Father, you have blessed us far beyond our deserving. We bow down before you in humility and thanksgiving: for this day and all that it means to us; for moments of silence when the soul could aspire to things lofty and sublime; for every noble influence that could touch our hearts and transform our lives; for the inspiring and abiding presence of him at whose table we are now gathered; for the host unseen with whom we are united in the communion of the saints; for those in times past who have held dear the vision of a militant Church, triumphant in your eternal Kingdom. Through their example revive in us such faith as will nerve our deepest desires in your service, and rekindle that hope that will lift the vision of the weary heart to eternity. This we pray especially for those among us who are in bereavement, giving you thanks with them for Christ who brought immortality to light and in whom there is the hope of life eternal.

O Lord, who has fashioned the destinies of mankind, we would commend to your care all who are in places of authority to lead and to govern. May their positions be to them a summons to humility of service. Through them may high resolve and dependence upon you lead us in the spirit of greatness-even in the service of your Kingdom. Give us, we pray, unity and brotherhood on the face of the earth. Check within all human beings the desires that make for bloodshed: the lust for power and the striving for dominion. Bestow on the leaders of the world the determination and patience that make for peace.

And may what we do here around your table increase within us such knowledge and grace that through us godliness, love, and mercy may convey your presence into the common place of our existence.

And to your name be honor, praise, and thanksgiving for ever....Amen.

4

Almighty God, your presence in the universe around us is beyond our understanding. The temples made by the hands of men are unworthy of your greatness and majesty. Nevertheless, we thank you that you are willing to dwell in humble and contrite hearts.

Therefore, O most merciful Lord, do we confess that often we are unworthy of your divine and fatherly love extended to us. Our response has often been without the devotion and commitment required of us. Sometimes our arrogance makes us oblivious of your goodness and unworthy citizens of your Kingdom. It is so easy to let our selfishness exceed our concern for our fellow human beings. Our pettiness often leads us to discrimination. Pardon us, we pray, our many shortcomings that obscure your presence from our hearts and in our lives.

Most gracious heavenly Father, in spite of our shortcomings, we thank you that your love is always manifested to us, if we would but look, that your providence has been our protection, and that your fatherhood can be our confidence. In the midst of war and violence in so many places in the world, we give thanks for the promise of peace on earth and for the

148

assurance left to us by Jesus Christ, "My peace I leave you, my peace I give unto you." We thank you that no temporal concern, or adversity is ever greater than the peace which you have in store for your own.

O God, you are the source of every good and perfect gift and we acknowledge our complete dependence upon you. As you dwell in us, bestow upon us, your people, the spiritual gifts that will transform us. Grant us tranquility from within and harmony with our own fellow human beings, that through us the day may be hastened when strife shall cease, and when war shall not be waged any more.

Let kindness and compassion motivate our thoughts, our speech, and our actions. Where there is hatred, we would bring peace; where there is tension, we would bring understanding; where there is mistrust, we would be instruments of confidence in one another. Enable us to convey what is divine into the everyday walks of life so that the presence of your Kingdom may become more real in the world around us.

And to your great name be honor and thanksgiving, always....Amen.

5

O God, you are the hope of all who truly seek you and the joy of all unto whom you reveal yourself. To you must all people come and before you must every knee bow. In you do we find and put our trust.

The thought of your holiness and love puts us to shame and, therefore, from you do we seek pardon. We are prone to evil and often we are reluctant to commit ourselves to what we know to be your sovereign and righteous will. With us often rests the blame for anxiety and peril that afflict people and nations in the world. In overconfidence we seek to fashion our own destinies and the destinies of mankind, and so many times we fail, for we seek what is expedient for a day, and abandon what is profitable for generations; and we put material gain above the interests of your Kingdom. Too many times our efforts have been lacking to bring to the nations the essential message to love you with heart, soul, and mind, and their neighbors as themselves.

Most gracious Father, we thank you that despite all our failures, there is always life in your Church and in any communion that seeks to serve you. We thank you for the wholesome influences that have permeated many places in the world, and are still doing so today; for many who count their lives as nothing unless they are spent in your service. Whatever they purpose in your name, bring to a glorious fruition, we pray.

Almighty God, we are grateful that you determine the destinies of mankind and of the nations, but you do not leave us without accountability. To all who are entrusted with grave decisions, grant wisdom, counsel, and your divine guidance. Turn the hearts of people from their foolish ways of prejudice and self-interest to understanding and self-sacrifice. Give us the confidence, we pray, that in your great goodness, you will overrule in the crises that continually beset nations.

And for our own responsibilities in your Kingdom, equip us with your whole armor that we may be steadfast, girded with your truth, equipped with the breastplate of righteousness, our feet shod with the preparation of the Gospel of peace. So guide us along the royal highway of your divine purpose, walking and working in faith, waiting with our eyes fixed on the horizon of hope, seeing the unseen.

And to you, Almighty God, be all dominion, and power for ever....Amen.

6

Almighty and everlasting God, you are the light of the ages that shone in the past, is still shining, and that will continue to illumine our hearts and our world. We thank you that in the love of Jesus Christ you have made your light a reality in the darkness of the world.

Merciful Lord, as your light shines in us, it convicts us of sin and compels us to confess: At times we excuse our wavering, condone our slothfulness, and seek to be ministered to, instead of to serve; we expect to be consoled, but are slow to comfort others. We thank you that your redeeming love comforts us in our boldness of confession to you, and assures us of forgiveness.

Our heavenly Father, accept, we pray, the gratitude of our hearts, so often beyond the ability of our minds and our lips: for the multitude of your gifts to us, many times undeserved; for the abundance of material things that pave our way of life; for the assurance of your truth and love that sustains us from day to day; for loved ones; for fellowship one with another, and above all with you.

We thank you for the splendor of your creation that brings us a message of your might and your power; for the light of this day that reminds us of the light and the beauty of holiness that comes from you and that must dwell in us.

Hear our prayer, O Lord, for the members of this fellowship. Grant them the grace to work while it is day, fulfilling diligently and patiently whatever duty is assigned to them; doing small things in the days of small things and performing great labors, if you should summon them to any; rising and working, or sitting still and waiting for your command. Minister to their every need from the treasures of your bounty. Bless every member. Enkindle your love in the heart of everyone whom you have called into this fellowship. Grant wisdom in days of testing, clarity of mind and the security that is rooted in the knowledge that we need not be ashamed of our stewardship into which you have called all who seek to serve you.

Hear our prayer, O Lord, and if it be your will, use us in your service for the coming and establishing of your Kingdom, and for the glory of your great name....Amen.

7

Memorial Service

Almighty God, our Father, from you we come and to you we return at the end of our days. We are here to call to mind the life of our loved one and our friend who has now departed from us to the life beyond.

We shed a tear, but nevertheless, we thank you that she (he) had been vouchsafed the privilege to be part of humanity, part of the wonders of our times, and part of your matchless creation to enjoy the marvels, the beauty, and the mysteries of your handiwork-the glory of many sunrises, the splendor of many sunsets, the sparkling of the restless seas that encompass us, the majesty of the mountains that you have set as sentinels of our planet. We thank you that her (his) eyes could rest on the wonder of the tenderness of the flowers of spring, the fullness of summer green, the masterful canvass of autumn, and the serenity of the winter landscape, the dazzling array of the starry host, lighting their lamps across the sky at eventide-forerunners of worlds beyond and beyond.

And now, Lord, our Father, as she (he) has been enveloped by the hush of eternity beyond, and as the rustle of her (his) footsteps will no longer sound among us, we thank you that her (his) work in this world has not been in vain. Annul the effects of any failures, if there were any. Although now gone from us, continue to establish, we pray, her (his) labors among us.

O God, who gives life and who summons it back home at your appointed time, who favored us with the hope of life eternal, in your omnipotence, and in your endless mercy, fulfill for our loved one and for ourselves also, the yearning of eternal life that throbs in every heart, lest we have labored and believed in vain and our footsteps disappear in quicksands of time.

And so, O great giver and sustainer of life, although now having set sail from the shores of eternity, may she (he) live on in the hearts of her (his) loved ones, in the fond memories of friends, but above all with you in eternity.

O Father of compassion, the great comforter of all, we commend to you those who now face an empty chair, an empty bedroom, the absence of a rustling footstep, and a voice, silent forever. Undergird them with your presence and your everlasting arms. As the brevity and frailty of life is made real to us, teach us so to number our days that we shall apply our hearts unto wisdom, always prepared ourselves to set sail from these shores on the oceans of eternity.

Hear us, O Lord, and hallow our moments of silent tribute, we pray....Amen.

8

Advent / Christmas

Almighty God, our Father, we join our hearts in gladness this day at church bells and even rusty plowshares, ringing out all over the face of the earth from the rising of the sun far to the east until it will set in the distant west, summoning the faithful, joyful and triumphant, to come, to bow down and to worship you.

We thank you for this hallowed season of Advent and Christmas with the unmistakable message: You do pierce the veil that separates us from your majesty to reveal yourself in the common place of life. You do indeed come to us with the supernatural, the miraculous, and the amazing. We humble ourselves to thank you for so manifesting yourself in the tenderness of the little child of Bethlehem-no crib for his bed-, in the rugged voice of John the Baptist, crying in the wilderness, "Prepare the way of the Lord," in the unique life of Jesus of Nazareth, and in a cross on a hill far away.

Hear Our Prayers And Hymns, O Lord, We Pray

We rejoice in the gifts of music and song, sacred and secular, with which we can celebrate this festive season. May they lift our spirits above the mundane things of our lives to what is unseen and eternal, and grant that we shall always hold these and the spirit of Christmas dear in our hearts.

As we worship together today, we miss and commend to your care all those not present with us, but confined to their beds or rooms because of frailty, and others because of illness and pain. Our hearts also go out with love to those among us who are bearing a cross of an incurable disease. We would bear their crosses with them that they may be light. We thank you for the advancement in numerous ways to minister to all of them, for the age of miracle medicines and undreamt of surgery. We especially thank you for those who are dedicated to research in our quest to conquer diseases.

As in spirit we join the happy throngs the world over, assembled and united in worship this day, we earnestly commend to you your Church wherever it is found, and especially this fellowship. Despite the great diversity of the Church, we thank you for the measure of unity under the umbrella of your love, the wideness of your mercy, and the presence of your Kingdom of which we have been vouchsafed to be citizens.

And as we depart from worshiping you this day, grant that there shall always remain in our hearts an everlasting song of love, faith, and hope that we may face the challenges of each day, even as Jesus Christ did, with courage, determination, leading us to victory.

Daniel J. Theron

And to your great name be all honor, glory, praise, and especially thanksgiving for the coming of the Prince of Peace....Amen.

DEDICATIONS OF OFFERINGS

1

Lord, our God, the whole earth and all the fullness thereof belong to you: the forests on a thousand hills, the grain in the valleys around us; the sheep and the cattle on the plains; the riches of the oceans encompassing us; and the treasures deep in the bosom of the earth below us. From the bounty with which you have so generously supplied us, we offer and we dedicate but a small portion as a token of our own rededication to you. Use our small gifts, we pray, and turn them into mustard seeds that they may grow to further and to establish your Kingdom on earth....Amen.

2

Our Father, Creator, you have summoned us in this world to be sowers and you have entrusted to us a great variety of seeds to sow along the way of life. Some fell on rocks, some on barren earth, but some did fall on fertile soil and brought forth forty-, sixty-, and one hundredfold. From the yield of our sowing and our labors we offer and dedicate to you only small portions as tokens of our devotion and gratitude to you. Use them, we pray, as seeds that they may grow to further your work in the world and to make your Kingdom more real in the hearts of your people. For the glory and praise of your great name we bring this offering....Amen.

3

Our Father, your providence and your fatherhood extend to us far beyond our merits and our deserving. We ask for our daily bread and you give us so much more: love, redemption, salvation, and the bread of life. Out of the material bounty with which you have favored us we consecrate to you a portion. We seek neither reward, nor return for the little that we give, but in faith we would cast our offering like bread on the waters of the world that it may return in the hearts of your people and on earth in the fullness of your Kingdom....Amen.

4

Lord, our God, to all of us you have entrusted a multitude of talents-to some ten, to some five, to some only one or two. From the investments and earnings of our talents we bring but a small fraction, a token of our own devotion and consecration to you. As we stand before you seeking your face, grant, we pray, that our offerings shall bring forth things that money can not buy, the unseen and the eternal-love, faith, and hope that lead us to life everlasting. And to your great name be all honor, and praise, and thanksgiving for ever....Amen.

5

Almighty God, you have provided for us like a true Father. You have set the hills and mountains around us as sentinels, made them of rocks, and covered them with forests that we may have material to build our homes.

You have carved out the valleys and filled them with fertile soil that they may bring forth abundantly for man and for beast.

You have stretched out the plains that herds and flocks may roam.

You have hidden treasures deep in the bosom of the earth, stored for our use.

We merely return part of what by your mercy we could earn from what you have entrusted to us to find. To you, giver of all, we bring these our offerings with rededication of ourselves and with thanksgiving in our hearts....Amen.

BENEDICTIONS

1

Our God, our inspiration, set your minds and hearts:
On whatsoever is true,
On whatsoever is honorable,
On whatsoever is just.
The Lord most holy inspire and direct you:
To whatsoever is pure,
To whatsoever is lovely,
To whatsoever is gracious
That you may ever grow in grace and holiness.
Amen. (Based on Philippians 4 : 8)

2

The Lord Almighty fill you with all knowledge,
All understanding and wisdom,
Enable you to lead a life well-pleasing to him,
To bear fruit in every good work.
The Lord turn your disappointments into Steppingstones to new destinies today and always.
The Lord give your life a new meaning beginning today.
Amen.

3

The Lord of all mercies and inspiration bestow upon you
His love that will undergird you,
Great faith that will sustain you,
Joy that will make you cheerful,

Courage that will dare the unthinkable,
Charity that will embrace those in need,
Peace that will surpass all understanding,
Hope that will see beyond the horizons of this
life.
Amen.

4

The Lord bless you and keep you.
The Lord equip you with his whole armor,
Undergird you with his truth,
Protect you with the breastplate of righteousness,
Shelter you from flaming darts with the shield of
faith,
Crown you with the helmet of salvation,
That you may be a worrier, worthy of his Kingdom.
Amen. (Based on Ephesians 6 : 14f.)

5

The Lord Almighty grant you the strength
to labor on each day:
For whatsoever is excellent,
For whatsoever is worthy of praise,
For whatsoever is up building,
For whatsoever is to the glory of his excellent
name,
Today and always.
Amen.(Based on Philippians 4 : 8)

6

The Lord provide you with the shield of faith,
Equip you with the Gospel of peace,
Make your feet swift to bring good tidings,

Make you strong in the struggle of life,
And for his honor, praise, and glory
Render you victorious to the end.
Amen. (Based on Ephesians 6 : 14 -17)

7

The Lord grant you strength
to overcome obstacles in your life,
Inspiration to fulfill your life's calling to his glory.
The Lord turn the darkness around you into sunshine,
Grant you vision of hope,
Enable you to see beyond the mist of the valleys,
Equip you to labor for his Kingdom while it is day,
Even today, and always.
Amen.

8

The love and protection of God our Creator and our Father,
The grace and salvation of Jesus Christ, our Redeemer,
The fellowship of God as Holy Spirit,
Remain with you to sanctify you and inspire you
this day and throughout your pilgrimage of life.
Amen.

9

The Lord be your good shepherd,
Lead you in peace to green pastures,
Refresh you by still waters in the heat of the day,
Restore your soul,

Direct you in the paths of righteousness.
The Lord be your companion all the days of your
life
That you may dwell in his house forever.
Amen. (Based on Psalm 23)

10

The Lord prepare a table
before you under all conditions of life,
Be it sorrow or gladness.
The Lord cause your cup to run over.
His goodness and mercy follow you
all the days of your life.
The Lord be your rod and your staff
in the valley of the shadow of death.
The Lord grant you salvation
to dwell in his mansions forever.
Amen.
(Based on Psalm 23)

11

The Lord our God endow you with a spirit of wisdom,
Enlighten you with insight to solve
the problems of life that confront you,
Make you vigilant against temptation that lies in
ambush on your way.
The Lord empower you to do his good works,
The Lord anoint you as an ambassador
of his Kingdom on earth,
And prepare you to be a citizen
in his Kingdom to come.
Amen.

12

The Lord make you as young as the rainbow.
The Lord grant you abundance of opportunities:
That your hands may do his work in the world,
That your ears would hear the cries for help,
That your eyes may see needs of others around you,
That your mouth would utter prayers for all people.
Amen.
(Based on the Civitan Creed)

13

The Lord endow you with a heart that beats for
every friend,
A heart that bleeds for every injury to humanity,
And throbs with joy at every triumph of truth.
A heart that knows no fear, but its own
unworthiness.
The Lord prepare your mind, and your heart
To be a good citizen,
To build good citizenship in the world,
Always ready to serve him by serving others.
And in the end the Lord provide you
A dwelling place in eternity.
Amen. (Based on the Civitan Creed)

14

The Lord, Almighty, precede you on the rest of your
pilgrimage through life that begins today,
Make pleasant the valleys before you,
Increase your strength to climb hills and mountains
that confront you.
His presence be a lamp unto your feet,
lest you stumble and fall.
The Lord shield you from the arrow that flies by
night,
The Lord avert the pestilence that walk in
darkness,
Grant you great faith, courage to dare,
And peace that passes all understanding.
Amen.

When the crooked is not made straight,
The Lord be your compass, lest you lose your way;
When the rough places are not made plain,
The Lord give you shoes to walk without pain or
fear;
When the mountains are too steep,
The Lord supply you with his staff of faith to
climb and to reach the summits;
When all fails and there seems to be no hope,
The Lord grant you wings to mount up like eagles!
Amen.

LYRICS

Pilgrims of Love, Faith, and Hope

I.

Daniel J. Theron

Old One Hundredth

Come, pil-grims, on-ward joy-ful-ly! Let love your in-spir-a-tion be!

Let faith pro-vide your staff and stay! Raise high hope's torch to light your way!

168

II. Love

Daniel J. Theron   *Old One Hundredth*

1. O God of love, come and im-part Your love to fill the wav'-ring heart.
2. So may love rule in us each day To face what-ev-er comes our way,
3. Let love in us be firm and strong To o-ver-come the lure of wrong,

Make us re-fined, meek, and be-nign, For love is gen-tle and di-vine.
Seek-ing to work God's will in us; To be our source of god-li-ness.
To tri-umph o-ver vi-o-lence, To bring our world the gift of peace.

4. Love's pow-er-ful, and never weak.
   It's strength can turn the other cheek.
   If we would change our wrongs to right,
   It will forgive, also forget.

5. Love is a friendship that's aflame;
   Through good and bad it stays the same.
   It makes up where we sometimes fail,
   For love's so strong, it will prevail!

6. Love is the spring of loyalty;
   Fills hearts with its integrity.
   Love is the source of faithfulness.
   It feeds the root of trust in us.

169

7. Love's humble, fount' of gratitude;
   It's thoughtful, kind, and never rude.
   Love is to be considerate.
   Love is to be compassionate.

8. Love sows the seeds of charity;
   Helps those who suffer poverty.
   Wherev'r love's touch the broken mends,
   It bonds a fellowship of friends.

9. Where love is, humor will be found;
   There laughter, bliss, and joy abound.
   If love would truly dwell in us,
   It shall fill life with happiness.

10. Love is a crown of thorns to wear.
    Love is my sister's cross to bear;
    Pays up my brother's penalty.
    Love is the door to liberty.

11. Love clears our hearts of worldliness;
    Creates a robe of godliness.
    Let love inspire us to life's end,
    To guide us to the world beyond.

III. Faith

Daniel J. Theron

Finlandia
Jean Sibelius

1. Faith is a bond, di - vine, with God a - bove. It's man - kind's
2. Faith is the power that stirs re - solve in us. Be there in
3. Faith is our strength through toil and tears of life; Our aid and

bond of fel - low - ship and love. Faith is how we be -
life des - erts and streams to cross. Faith in our hearts will
staff in suf - fer - ing and pain. It is our shield to

lieve what we be - lieve. Let faith in - spire life's pur - pose ev - 'ry
ban - ish threats of fear, I - deals and dreams, im - pos - si - ble, to
shel - ter us in strife; When sun - set comes, faith's com - fort will re -

day: For it's our strength to la - bor and a -
dare. Faith kin - dles hope what fu - ture years may
main. When at life's end we're called to leave this

chieve. Our sure sup - port, our stead - fast staff and stay.
be; Nerves us to strive and reach our des - ti - ny.
earth, Faith lib - er - ates from dread and sting of death.

171

Daniel J. Theron

IV. Hope

Daniel J. Theron

Finlandia
Jean Sibelius

1. Hope is a gift from God di – vine to us, Our source of
2. Hope lifts our hearts to be un – bound and free. Vi – sions be –
3. Rain – bows of hope will fol – low storms and rain. And tem – pest's
4. When at last breaks hope's dis – tant tri – umph song On pil – grim's

strength when we are in dis – tress. It is the eye of faith that sees be –
yond and vis – tas far to see. Helps us en – dure 'til vi – sions will be
gloom will ear – ly change to blue. They cov – e – nant that soon the sun will
ear, a – wait – ed for so long. Rest in God's love when jour – ney's end has

yond Gives con – fi – dence in what will be or – dained;
real. And nerves our will to reach our dis – tant goal.
shine Hope is our dreams we dream will soon come true.
come Clutch your staff, faith, for it will help you home

Keeps our hearts stout to walk our pil – grim's way.
Yet, hope, our friend, could be our en – e – my!
Hope's vi – sion is our fi – nal des – ti – ny.
E – ter – ni – ty, where hope and faith and love.

172

Hope pierc - es night and guides to dawn and day.
If rea - son fails to see fu - til - i - ty.
For hope will lead us to e - ter - ni - ty!
Have guid - ed you to God who reigns a - bove!

Daniel J. Theron

Praise the Lord, the Almighty -
Psalm 146

Daniel J. Theron
Translated as based on the 1944 Afrikaans Hymnal

1. Praise the Lord with joy - ful voic - es; Ju - bi - lant his prais - es sing. As in him the world re - joic - es, I too will my trib - ute bring: Him who has so fav - ored me. Al - ways laud in mel - o - dy.

2. Have no faith in world - ly prin - ces in the end they're pow - er - less. For their life on earth is temp' - ral; So their might and pride will fall, Earth to earth and dust to dust, They're not wor - thy of your trust.

3. Bless - ed all who on life's jour - ney, Thirst - y, pressed by heat of day, Find - ing no sup - port or suc - cor, On - ly trust in God's great pow'r; Ev - en in the dark - est night Trust in God for dawn and light.

4. Praise the Lord who earth and heav - en Set in per - fect reg - i - men, All the crea - tures, land and o - ceans He did make and still sus - tains. We will trust his faith - ful - ness; For he keeps his prom - is - es.

5. Thanks to God, who to the needy
   In distress will send relief;
   Who will comfort in his mercy
   Those who languish in their grief;
   Minds those in captivity;
   Breaks their bonds and sets them free.

174

6. Thanks to God, whose tender mercies
   To the blind restore their eyes;
   He'll aid those in dust dejected.
   By his word they will be raised.
   He loves all who uprightly
   Seek to serve him faithfully.

7. God protects and guards the strangers,
   Watches over sojourners.
   Widows with their orphans grieving,
   He will help and comfort bring.
   He will be their staff and stay;
   Sends oppressors on their way.

8. God Almighty's pow'r is endless,
   Without end his faithfulness,
   Lord and mas-ter of the future,
   Monarch, reigning evermore.
   Zion, lift your voice and sing:
   Tribute, laud, and honor bring!

   (Music from and written with consultation of the
   1944 Afrikaans Hymnal)

God Over and In All

Daniel J. Theron
Translated as based on the 1944 Afrikaans Hymnal, Gesang 7

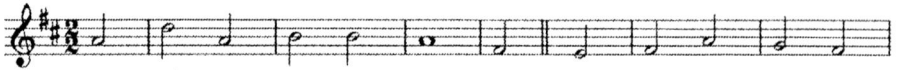

1.In val - ley and on moun - tain, And ev - ery - where is
2.God's pres - ence is all o - ver. He knows all far and
3.All that on land are teem - ing, Or in its wat - ers
4.Re - joice that our ex - is - tence Rests in the care of

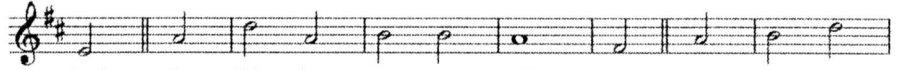

God In life where we so of - ten Are wan - d'ring,
near. Re - ly - ing on his pow - er Will han - ish
stay, Or through the skies are fly - ing, And with such
God: When aid in suf - f'ring fails us Our com - fort

there is God; Where - e'er our think - ing rang - es, A -
all our fear: For birds he makes a shel - ter. He
glad - ness play, Join with God's vast ex - pan - ses Pro -
comes from God; When hands of friends so faith - ful Can't

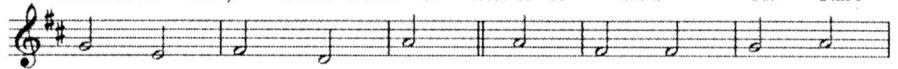

bove from sphere to sphere, E'en to the ut - most
decks the plains with grass. Pro - vides for all in
claim by day and night His nev - er end - ing
save us, there is God; In death when all is

reach - es, Yes, God is pre - sent there.
win - ter. He rules the u - ni - verse.
good - ness, His great - ness and his might.
peace - ful Our ref - uge is in God!

God's Goodness

Daniel J. Theron
Translation as based on the 1944 Afrikaans Hymnal, Gesang 12
(Stanzas 3 and 5 have been switched.)

1. God's good-ness pass - es un - der - stand-ing. Who is by it not
2. Who fash-ioned me so won - der - ful - ly? The God who has no
3. Would I to God no trib - ute of - fer? His good-ness fail to
4. It is my grat - i - tude, God's or - der, I must so strive un -

deep - ly moved? How thank-less is the hu - man be - ing
need of me. Who in his wis - dom guides me dai - ly?
laud and praise? Would I not lis - ten to his or - der?
-til I see Goals set for me so great and high - er,

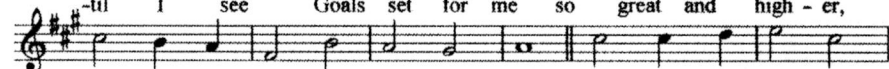

Who does not lift his heart to God. To whom should we thanks -
The God whose hand I fail to see. Who fills with peace my
Not wish to fol - low in his ways? No, Lord, you rule my
Un - til his stat - ure forms in me. If I could see my

giv - ing ren - der? Let this my song, my long - ing be:
in - ner be - ing? Who fills my heart with joy - ful song?
will, my striv - ing. In me your word in - grained will be:
pur - pose clear - ly, I could at - tain what I must be.

My soul, the Lord your God re - mem - ber,
Who show - ers me with his full bless - ing,
It's lov - ing you with all my be - ing,
If I would love the Lord more dear - ly,

For he will ev - er think of me.
The God of love and grace so strong.
Like - wise, my neigh - bor just like me.
Then e - vil will not rule in me.

5. Think, O my soul, of life hereafter,

Your home beyond where you belong.

Where your abode, lasting forever,

Will be in glory still unsung.

Rejoice, my soul, in expectation.

God dearly wrought eternal life:

The price was Jesus' crucifixion;

We're free from debt of sin and strife.

6. Then, Holy Spirit, may your presence,
   My inspiration ever be:
   To consecrate all to your service,
   To strengthen high resolve in me;
   Support to me in times of suff'ring,
   My comfort in anxiety,
   Even with joy to be awaiting
   Commencement of eternity.

(Music from and written with consultation of the 1944 Afrikaans Hymnal, Gesang 12. Stanzas 3 and 5 have has been switched.)

Peace in the Midst of Change

Daniel J. Theron
Translated as based on the 1944 Afrikaans Hymnal, Gesang 22

1. Peace, my soul, your Lord is rul - er; All cre - a - tion's
2. For the new to come we're la - b'ring. Yet, we long for
3. Peace, my soul, your Lord is rul - ing. Be con - tent what -

his do - main. What may change is by the
what has been; Still, for what is gone we're
e'er your lot. No - tice how the world is

or - der Of him who'll the same re - main.
crav - ing; Long - ing for what's still un - seen.
chang - ing, And de - pend a - lone on God.

179

O! America

Daniel J. Theron

George William Warren

1. O! Land of splen - dor, love - ly to be -
2. Land, where our roots tapped deep through cen - tu -
3. O! Land of hope for mil - lions in the
4. Beau - ti - ful land, so blessed by Prov - i -

hold: Guard - ed by break - ers ju - bi - lant and
ries, Midst pas - tures, grain, ma - chines, and fac - to -
past, Quilt - ed in cus - toms, faiths, and ways so
dence With trea - sures grand, a - dorned and so im -

bold, Cra - dled se - rene - ly in sun - burst and
ries, We sing with praise and joy and grat - i -
vast, Spread o - ver cit - y, moun - tain, plain, and
mense, We cher - ish all that you're pro - vid - ing

plain, Might - y in moun - tains, pride of your do -
tude, Of pi - o - neers in - spired with for - ti -
vale, In har - mo - ny that friend - ship may pre -
us; We shall o - bey your call to no - ble -

main;
tude,
vail;
ness.

With wind, and breeze, and bird this song we
Be - cause on free - dom's rock they built our
Con - trast of all cre - a - tion's won - der -
In broth - er - hood we grasp each oth - ers

raise;
land:
ment,
hand;

Be - lov - ed land, to you we sing our praise.
On truth's foun - da - tion you will al - ways stand.
Our des - ti - ny one na - tion and one land.
To - geth - er we shall march for you, Dear Land!

Chorus (with first and last stanzas only)

O! our Dear Land, our prayers as - cend for you!

We'll dream and hope, and sac - ri - fice for you!

END OF TEXT AND BOOK, HEAR OUR PRAYERS , O LORD....

181

ABOUT THE AUTHOR

Daniel J. Theron was born in the Orange Free State in the Republic of South Africa. He grew up in the southeastern Transvaal, went to school at Greylingstad and Standerton High School, and graduated from the University of Pretoria, A. B., M. A., and B. D. in the Theological Faculty, Section B. He was Lecturer in the Department of Classics at the University of Pretoria.

He received a Th./Ph.D. Degree from Princeton Theological Seminary with a thesis on Paul's Concept of Truth....Here he served on the faculty for several years during the 1940s and 1950s, in the New Testament division.

He was ordained in the Presbyterian Church U. S. A.

He is the author of several books and articles, *Evidence of Tradition....*, a text book for graduate students in New Testament and Patristic Studies, several articles on the theology of the Apostle Paul, a number of other articles, many book reviews, and *Out of Ashes, The Boers' Struggle for Freedom during the English War of 1899-1902*.

He is also well versed in finances, spent many years in the investment business, and still continues his interest in this field, He has always been writing, and has several manuscripts in their final stages.

He served as chaplain for many years, especially in the service club organization of Civitan International.

Printed in the United States
5214